The
Southern Way

The regular volume for the Southern devotee

Kevin Robertson

Issue 40

www.crecy.co.uk

© 2017 Crécy Publishing Ltd
and the various contributors

ISBN 978 190932 8648

First published in 2017 by Noodle Books
an imprint of Crécy Publishing Ltd

All editorial submissions to:
The Southern Way (Kevin Robertson)
Conway
Warnford Rd
Corhampton
Hants SO32 3ND
Tel: 01489 877880
editorial@thesouthernway.co.uk

Publisher's note: Every effort has been made to
identify and correctly attribute photographic
credits. Any error that may have occurred is
entirely unintentional.
In line with the new design the front cover image has
changed from that originally advertised. All other
information is unaffected.

Printed in England by LatimerTrend

Noodle Books is an imprint of
Crécy Publishing Limited
1a Ringway Trading Estate
Shadowmoss Road
Manchester M22 5LH

www.crecy.co.uk

Issue No 41 of THE SOUTHERN WAY
ISBN 978 190932 8747
available in January 2018 at £14.95
To receive your copy the moment it is
released, order in advance from your usual
supplier, or it can be sent post-free (UK)
direct from the publisher:

Crécy Publishing Ltd

1a Ringway Trading Estate, Shadowmoss
Road, Manchester M22 5LH

Tel 0161 499 0024

www.crecy.co.uk

enquiries@crecy.co.uk

Front Cover:
Early days at the Bluebell with their 'E4' No 32473
(originally LBSCR No 473 *Birch Grove*) at Horsted
Keynes. Built in 1898, the engine was withdrawn at the
end of October 1962 and immediately purchased for
preservation. It was quickly repainted into Marsh livery
so this view is from the brief period after purchase from
BR and before repainting.

Rear cover:
'M7' No 30108 at Thorneycroft's siding, Basingstoke,
with the REC 'Rambling Rose' tour of 23 March 1963.
Trevor Owen/Hugh Davies

Title page:
Regular readers will likely be thinking the editor is
obsessed with snow ploughs. Be assured, not a bit of it. I
am aware we have had several odd pieces of relevance
to the subject but every so often something new comes
up which warrants inclusion. Here is one example, 'Q'
No 30548 outside the front of Eastleigh Works either
ready prepared for work or perhaps about to be
restored to normal condition. This particular engine was
one the last three members of the class, the others
being No 30535 at Salisbury and 30545 at Nine Elms. All
were fitted out for snow plough duty, No 30548 also
being used on local freight work. The end finally came
for No 30548 in the spring of 1965 at which time and
according to Bradley, the engine had covered 484,004
miles in just under 26 years, or something in the order
18,600 miles a year. *Roger Thornton`*

Contents

Editorial

I suspect July of this year created more than a little reflection in the minds of many. Fifty years since the end of steam, no more Bulleids, no more Standards, and no more green coaches with voluptuous springs which spread clouds of dust every time posterior came into contact with moquette. I won't recount what I was doing back then; we will all have our individual memories, suffice to say it seemed to me to be the end of an era, as indeed it was. Somehow I had convinced myself that it just could not come to an end so suddenly, but it did of course, and the railways of the sixties are indeed gone forever – as indeed are the seventies, eighties and so on.

So where do we go from here and by that I mean with SW? Well, if I am honest I never thought that 10 years on from the Preview issue I would be sat at a computer screen on a glorious summer's day preparing Issue No 40. In all seriousness I felt at the time that the idea of 'A Regular Journal for the Southern devotee' was worth pursuing and to that end and to hopefully to create the 'Wow' factor invested in excess of £1,000 in a few images from the commercial picture libraries. Whether that was right or not and indeed whether it had the desired effect is history, I made mistakes, but I also had the privilege of speaking to and in many cases meeting a wonderful band of likeminded enthusiasts who were only too keen to open up their own archives and allow material to be used. Sadly, some are no longer with us and we are all the poorer for that.

In having charge of the compilation of 'SW' I also have the responsibility of selecting the articles to appear therein. The bonus is that I get to read them before deciding and let me say also that I am forever grateful to every last one of those contributors whether it be a one-off piece or something sent by one of our regulars. Rarely have I rejected anything although sometimes I will admit the filing system is perhaps not quite as good as it should be and therefore some can be totally and unintentionally delayed.

I have never set a definite timescale so far as the period of coverage that applies to each issue is concerned. I will admit that the original idea was say 1900 to 1970 but, as readers will be aware, we have strayed outside those dates from time to time in a similar way that on occasions non-SR topics have appeared. (Every time a non-Southern image or article is featured, even a single photograph, I await the brickbats although they are actually fewer than I might have expected.) What I will say is that when I or a contributor gets it wrong you are quick to point it out and for that we must also be grateful. I well recall a conversation with Paul Karau of Wild Swan many years ago when he had just started *Great Western Journal* and asking him if he was going to do the same for the Southern? This was back in the 1980s, in the days when I had a 'proper job' and the thought of ever being a publisher let alone producing something like 'SW' had not crossed my mind. Paul's reply was to the effect that whilst there were a number of Great Western experts, the Southern was such a vast concern comprising so many different aspects that he did not feel there was a single person with enough knowledge to do it justice. That person is certainly NOT me, not then and not now, but I will tell you who it is and that is YOU, every last one of you. You contribute the articles, the images, the corrections and the suggestions. Truth be told we are all likely experts in a few very specialist areas. No one can know everything but I continue to have the deepest respect for those who can sprout chapter and verse on their speciality, Southern or otherwise. They are the ones with their respective contributions who make 'SW' what it is. As I mentioned earlier I just have the privilege of reading these and enhancing my own knowledge in the same way as I am sure everyone will gain something – even if it is just a refresher!

So in answer as to where we go from here, I would suggest more of the same. Just because we have reached a particular milestone does not mean we cannot include more mementoes from the past, and I look forward very much to seeing what the email and/or the post delivers in the future.

Finally, as I was preparing this issue I learnt of the sad passing of Bert Moody of Southampton, author of several railway and shipping books including the excellent *Southampton's Railways*. Bert was well into his 90s and was a much appreciated mentor to the present author in his own studies of the railways in the local area.

Kevin Robertson

Smoke Deflectors for SR Steam Locomotives

John Harvey

On the penultimate day of Southern Steam operation in 1967, the writer recalls standing at Dorchester South station watching the departure of one of the last steam-hauled Bournemouth-bound trains. He was joined by a gentleman who introduced himself as an engineman. 'Don't know why I bothered to come', he said referring to the locomotive, 'I hate the things'. Surprised at such sentiments on this particular day, which for many was akin to a funeral, an occasion where it is usual that only laudatory remarks are directed towards the deceased, the writer was puzzled and asked the perhaps obvious question, 'Why?'

After making an unsolicited excuse for his attendance and apologising for taking a snapshot of such an ill-begotten device for pulling a train, the engineman questioned the intelligence of designers who produced machines that did everything they

The standard Urie 'N15', represented here by No 737 built at Eastleigh in 1918 and likely recorded soon after introduction. (In subsequent SR days the engine was named *King Uther*.) The engine is fitted with a short chimney – likely the tallest that could be accommodated within the loading gauge. It is seen in what was then Platform 3 at Eastleigh with a down Bournemouth line train and judging from its pristine condition probably not long after entering service.

could to make the operators life as difficult as possible. 'Look at all that smoke, ash and grit being pumped out, right in the driver's face', he added.

Confused by the mixture of emotions, the writer felt that it was better to let the conversation die in preference to his memory of the Bulleid Pacific that had, a few minutes before, stormed up the bank from Weymouth to Bincombe tunnel. Nevertheless, the engineman had a point and although his remarks had been generally directed at all steam locomotives from the *Rocket* onwards, critics of Bulleid's work point to smoke clearance as one of the major faults of the Pacifics. The fact that Bulleid's 'Leader' was but one of the comparatively few steam engine designs to arrange that the exhaust left the locomotive at a position *behind* that of the driver, so providing a clear view forward, seems largely to have escaped the attention of commentators. *(This got me thinking, and I believe John to be 100% correct [in the UK], unless one includes the odd experimental design where the driver sat in a forward compartment. There were, though, two notable exceptions; firstly the obvious when running tender/bunker first, and secondly so far as the steam-railmotor design was concerned, and where the driver's cab was, when running forward, positioned ahead of the chimney. We discount pull-push/auto trains. – Ed.)*

Students of SR locomotive history will no doubt be aware of the wind tunnel tests that were carried out on a model of a 'Merchant Navy', and of the various modifications that were made during and after the war to improve smoke and steam clearance. Yet how many know that similar wind tunnel tests were carried out in 1931 on the 'Schools' class locomotives, a design that is generally regarded for its excellence, consistently attracting favourable comments? The point is that the problems with smoke clearance arose not from the foibles of an individual designer, but essentially from requirements to produce more powerful and more efficient locomotives hauling faster and more comfortable trains for the benefit of the passenger.

The matter of coal consumption and thermal efficiency was not only something of interest to academics and the accountants who kept a watchful eye on the Company's coal bill. For example, Gresley's early Pacifics were not capable of taking a worthwhile train non-stop between London and Edinburgh because they could not carry enough coal: the problem was in essence solved not by building bigger tenders but by making the locomotives more efficient with long travel valves (giving lower cylinder exhaust steam pressure) so that they could do the work required within the capacity of the fuel on the tender. A different case which occurred in the 1950s concerned former GWR locomotives. The requirement to take lower quality coal combined with a need to reduce spark emissions caused performance difficulties and jeopardised express train timekeeping. Acceptable standards were regained through a programme of fitting larger superheaters and, in the case of the 'King' and 'County' classes and some 'Castle' class engines, the fitting of a double chimney. Higher boiler steam temperatures and lower cylinder exhaust pressures here served to improve thermal performance (particularly at higher speeds) whilst the improved draughting that resulted from the double blastpipe maintained the flow of air through the firebox in spite of both the greater quantities of ash than originally designed for and the restriction caused by spark arresters.

As an aside it is curious to note that the superheater surface was removed from the Bulleid Pacifics so reducing thermal efficiency at about the same time that the Western Region was finding benefit from an increase. Was this the real reason that the 'Merchant Navy' achieved a lower thermal efficiency than 'Britannia'? Maybe the 'as designed' general capability of the Bullied Pacifics to carry out their work did not demand the kind of performance improvements needed of the LNER Pacifics, the 'Castles' or the 'Kings'. After all, what was the importance of an extra hundredweight or two of coal due to thermal efficiency *when the engine was doing its job on the road?*

Probably not much. And so when we look back to the early months following the Grouping, we find that the SR needed (among many other things) more powerful engines to haul heavier trains *now*! To cut a long story short, Maunsell took the largest available existing design and developed that. The Urie 'H15' class 4-6-0s had proved their worth during World War 1, but the express passenger version, the 'N15' class, was disappointing because the locomotives were not capable of

sustaining the required power output. Experiments and modifications including increasing the valve travel and exhaust improvements would significantly improve both performance and efficiency, resulting in the physically similar 'King Arthur' class, a thoroughly satisfactory design.

But, there was one problem. The boiler and smokebox dimensions allowed only a short chimney to be fitted within the loading gauge (slightly shorter in fact than the Urie stovepipe chimneys of the 'N15'). When combined with the relatively soft (and efficient) exhaust that these engines worked in normal operation, steam and smoke frequently obscured the driver's view especially when heading directly into the prevailing wind – akin to all express services out of Waterloo as far as Woking, Bournemouth line trains as far as Woking, and West of England services all the way to Exeter. Although the reasons for this are manifold and complex, it is helpful to understand the main factors involved.

First the steam/smoke exhaust takes a divergent (spreading) conical form as it leaves the chimney. When the locomotive is moving slowly the cone is nearly vertical but as the engine speed increases the cone is curved backwards and may become horizontal. Depending on how hard the engine is working and the velocity of the exhaust compared with the speed of travel, the edge of the cone of steam and smoke may not clear the roof of the driver's cab and so obscure his lookout.

Similarly when a conventional steam locomotive moves at speed, the smokebox front forces the approaching air radically outwards away from smokebox. It is physically impossible for this air to change direction immediately at the periphery of the smokebox and follow the shape directly, but relatively slowly a change of direction does take place so that the bulk of the air that the engine displaces flows approximately parallel with the boiler surface, although at some distance from it. Between the flowing air and the boiler/smokebox surface there is a layer of 'dead' (or stagnant) air. This layer is sometimes quite thick and can occur, perhaps, in some surprising places around the locomotive. The phenomenon can be seen in a number of film clips of Bulleid Pacifics at speed: observe the top of the smokebox *ahead of the chimney* and a small cloud of steam can often be seen there moving along with the loco. Although the 'dead' air layer may contain a turbulent area, anything such as steam or smoke that enters it does not easily get out again unless there is a stream of air to make it do so. A side wind for example, may drive away the smoke/steam from one side of the engine, but when this happens matters tend to become worse on the other side. Where the cloud of steam can be seen in front of the chimney on a rebuilt Pacific, note also that the deflectors force clean air along the side of the smokebox, so sweeping any steam away and allowing the driver a forward view.

Now, in earlier years when express engines had relatively small smokeboxes and tall(er) chimneys (think of a 'T9'), the exhaust was usually projected with significant velocity beyond the 'dead' air and carried away in the passing air stream. In these circumstances the 'dead' air layer was not filled with exhaust and the driver's cab was usually surrounded by clean air. Think also of the LNER 'A4' design. Here the chimney top projects through this area of clean air and the conical exhaust is normally held clear of the cab, so maintaining the driver's view. The GWR 'Castles' and 'Kings' with their markedly tapered boiler design allowed for a sufficiently tall chimney on a smallish smokebox, hence these classes also project their exhaust outside of the 'dead' air layer and their cabs were not usually surrounded by steam and smoke.

However, the exhaust from locomotives with a large diameter smokebox and a short chimney may not be projected as far as the stream of air which naturally flowed past the locomotive, but in part at least into the 'dead' layer and along the firebox side to the cab windows, blocking the driver's view. When combined with the softer exhaust, which did not force the cone of smoke and steam so high and allow it to fall around the cab, the potential for poor visibility was high. The capuchon had offered some benefit, but loading gauge limitations reduced its size and consequently its effective properties. On the SR, the 'King Arthur' class was the first to suffer from these effects and drivers began to complain.

In a paper presented to the Institute of Locomotive Engineers in September 1941, Harold Holcroft described the work carried out to resolve this situation. The writer has drawn heavily on that paper and he gratefully acknowledges the fact. The Holcroft paper includes a number of drawings but so far as this article is concerned, photographs are used where possible.

Experimental Smoke Deflector Apparatus in the 1920s

Towards 1925, the need for a smoke clearing appliance became urgent and a number of experimental devices were tried. Several of these proposals were based on some form of scoop (one such was fitted to No E450 in February 1926, adjacent to the chimney and intended to divert the air into an upward direction and so lift the steam and smoke). Other suggestions were based on openings in or adjacent to the smokebox front with ducts conveying streams of air to the back of the chimney, analogous to the water pick-up apparatus on tenders.

Another proposal was that of levelling off the front of the smokebox to form a slope in advance of the chimney and fixing over this a curved bonnet, the intention being to give the air an upward direction by the slope and confine it from spreading by means of the bonnet so that a concentrated volume of air was projected below the back of the chimney.

Whether the fitting of an experimental louvred stovepipe chimney to No E755 was an attempt to improve smoke lifting or to reduce downdraught when the regulator was shut is not clear to the writer, but nevertheless the locomotive was so fitted at this time. No E457 also was fitted with a small device on the chimney. Holcroft reported that yet another design was to fix a shrouding on the front of the smokebox in the form of a semi-circular shelf. The object was to create a pocket of still air in front of the locomotive and thereby set up improved aerodynamic conditions: according to Bradley a device fitting this description was carried by No E753 from 21 May to 16 June 1926.

Coterminus with the 1926 trials taking place, similar experiments were also being made on the Continent and a satisfactory solution of the problem was reached on the German State Railways by the fixing of a vertical deflector plate on the edge of the platform on each side of the smokebox and slightly in advance of it. These plates prevent the lateral spread of a portion of the air displaced by the locomotive when in motion. By confining clean air in a channel parallel to the direction of travel with escape at the back and top only, these side plates reduce the amount of 'dead' air at the sides of the smokebox and boiler by diverting the air stream along it, so helping to keep the intervening distance to the cab windows clear of steam and smoke (as witnessed by the rebuilt Pacifics even when the smokebox top is shrouded in steam). While not fully effective under all conditions, these plates did improve matters and were considered well worth fitting on classes of engines where the smoke nuisance was really troublesome. In England such plates appeared first on the Southern Railway fitted to No E772 *Sir Percivale* in September 1926.

The 'scoop' or is it a form of 'wing plate' fitted to No E450 *Sir Kay*. In the Irwell Press *Book of the King Arthur 4-6-0s*, Richard Derry refers to this arrangement as somewhat reminiscent of Hermes, messenger of the gods, no doubt an apt description.

The wing plates fitted to No E772 *Sir Percival* in September 1926, displaying a distinct Continental appearance. The engine retained them until as late as October 1932.

The same fitting seen from the rear: again the seemingly flimsy appearance of the stays is apparent. *Rod Blencowe*

Although these 'German' plates gave good results, Holcroft states they left little foothold for the driver or others to pass from the running plate to the front of the engine being fixed near the edge of the platform. One may wonder if this is entirely correct as photographic evidence would suggest the opposite. Further, it was said that the height of the plates and the stays at the top partially obstructed the view from the cab, but visually the stays appear to have been shaped to allow access underneath them. Another quoted disadvantage was that it was necessary to take down the plates when drawing out piston valves for examination, although the plates eventually adopted suffered the same problem and for which a simple solution was later devised. A further argument, not without weight, was that the appearance of these plates was aesthetically disastrous.

Bradley has noted that No E450's scoop was removed after a few months so that it ran from March to December 1927 without any smoke deflecting equipment. We may conclude therefore that it was better off without the scoop! Also, Holcroft concludes that with the exception of the German plates, the general lack of any success with the experimental devices indicates that the theories on which they were based did not coincide with the true situation.

However, until satisfactory solutions to the problems were reached, numbers of suggestions poured in from drivers, firemen and others who were interested. This served to show that the trouble was an acute one and that a solution was urgent, at any rate so far as the Southern Railway was concerned. Among the ideas submitted was a semi-circular blower ring fixed at the back of the chimney for use when conditions were bad but this consumed a lot of valuable high-pressure steam without any resultant effect when on trial. (The writer wonders if this was the device fitted to No E457?)

Another idea was to fill in the intervening space between the chimney and dome with a casing of rectangular cross section, the object being to eliminate the low-pressure region behind the chimney and into which partial void the exhaust was drawn down on occasions.

Clearly at the beginning of 1927 the SR was not satisfied and more trials were carried out starting in March when No E783 (ex works on 6 March 1927) was fitted with a device that looked like an inverted shovel in front of the chimney.

Attempting to build on the comparative success of the German plates, a modified design was also made that was physically smaller and also set further inwards thus giving a better foothold (presumably a foothold *on the outside* is what is meant by Holcroft). The results from this less visually intrusive type fitted alongside the smokebox of No E453 (ex works on 2 April 1927) were definitely inferior, reports Holcroft, and it was evident that the extension forward of the smokebox front had an important bearing on the effectiveness of the plates.

Things were now happening quickly it seems, and a further modification appeared on No E779 when it left works on 16 April 1927. No E779's plates had a forward extension and a vertical joint which suggests that originally they had been made like No E453's but now had an additional forward section bolted on. This extension also had a markedly rounded top. Close study of photographs shows that these E779 plates were set slightly further towards the edge of the platform than E453's and those that would follow later. This resulted in the lack of any protrusion of the steampipe through the base of the deflector on this particular locomotive, the protrusion being evident on all other 'King Arthurs'.

Not yet content, Eastleigh fitted No E774 during its next general overhaul in June 1927 (ex works on 2 July) with a very

The 'inverted shovel' on No E783 *Sir Gillemere* with its March 1927 fitment. Mention must also be made of the somewhat flimsy plate fitted in the same position to No E753 *Melisande* which apart from being in the Bradford Barton book referred to in the text is also illustrated on p41 of *The Book of the King Arthurs*.

similar device to that which had been fitted to No E753 during May and June 1926 – might this have even been the same one? (See photograph dated August 1927 in the Bradford Barton *Southern Steam in Close Up* volume.) Further, Holcroft states that the type as first fitted to No E779 was a compromise design between No E453's and No E772's plates and although the results were not quite as good as with the 'German' type, they overcame many objections and represented the best all-round pattern, so becoming the standard for the 'King Arthurs'. In addition to being inset from the edge of the platform to improve access, suitable hand holds were provided to facilitate access to the front of the engine from the ground by way of footsteps. Also the lower section of the plates in front of the smokebox was now removable without the necessity of taking down the complete plate in order to facilitate access to the piston valves. A slight inward angle was also now given to the plates in order to attach them directly to the hand rails at the top.

General fitting of this compromise 'standard' design commenced in November 1927 and the majority of the 'King Arthur' class including the original 'N15s' had received deflectors by the end of 1929. All of the experimental deflectors were soon removed except for No E772, which retained the 'German' plates for six years and so became the last to receive standard plates when it emerged after overhaul in October 1932.

Winkworth records that in June 1929, approval was given for 61 engines of the 'H15' and 'S15' classes to be fitted with smoke deflectors. It is worth recording that Bradley gives 'H15'

No E523 as being equipped in April 1927 but an H. C. Casserley image dated 12 August 1928 shows the same engine without deflectors.

As Holcroft noted, setting the plates a few inches from the edges of the platforms to leave narrow ledges for a foothold caused some loss of effectiveness as they presented a narrower opening for the catchment of air. When it was decided to fit the 'Lord Nelson' class in 1929, with probably No E850 *Lord Nelson* being the first when ex-works on 18 May 1929, the catchment area compared with the 'King Arthur' type was slightly increased by setting the plates vertically and fixing them at the top with short stays clipped to the hand rails. The last five 'Lord Nelsons' to be built, Nos 861–865 in September–November 1929, all had smoke deflectors fitted during construction.

Uncertainty in 1930

A further matter worth noting is that photographic evidence shows that the 330 and 482 series of 'H15s' were fitted with the 'King Arthur' angled type of plates when the general fitting of smoke deflectors was commenced. Six engines so fitted have been identified: Nos E331–2, E483–4 and E487–9, the work being carried out between June 1929 and January 1930. No E485 has not been identified: the type of deflector and date fitted is not known. However, it must be assumed that even after the fitting of deflectors, complaints from drivers of these 'H15s' were still strong, because a change of policy on the type

The standard angled plates seen here fitted to No 755 *The Red Knight* depicted in wartime black livery.

of deflector to be fitted to these locos is evident from March 1930, when Nos E334 and E482 emerged from Eastleigh works with the vertical type. With the exception of No 491 (the odd one out with the 'King Arthur' boiler), all eventually received the vertical-type smoke deflectors similar to the 'Lord Nelsons'. This modification would seem to have been the only solution offering further, slight improvement available to the SR, short of expensive alterations to the front of the locomotive. With the benefit of hindsight, the massive smokeboxes and short chimneys of these 'H15' engines might have been expected to give the driver difficulties when they were being lightly worked.

Holcroft's acknowledgement that the compromise design was not wholly satisfactory is not only indicated by the changes made to the 'H15' deflectors during 1930, but also by a trial on No E773 of a device that had similarities with that previously carried on Nos E753 and E774. No E773 first received deflectors in December 1927, but the 'standard' design is not present in a comparatively distant view taken by H. C. Casserley in 1930 where the experiment appears as a forward extension of the upper half of the smokebox wrapper plate. Messrs Bradley and Nock also give 1930 as the date of this experiment.

The starting point for the wind tunnel tests and a comparison between boiler pitch and consequently chimney height between 'old' and 'modern' steam designs.

The Wind Tunnel Tests

Accordingly in 1931, tests on a model of a 'Schools' and also a 'U' class 2-6-0 were carried out and Holcroft's paper includes photographs of the model complete with exhaust streams. Several varying configurations, including those found successful in practice, were tested over a range of speed and exhaust velocity. Interestingly, a simple 'head board or destination disc', when carried on the 'bracket' (lamp-iron) at the top of the smokebox was found to offer some benefit with less smoke passing along the sides of the boiler and around the cab.

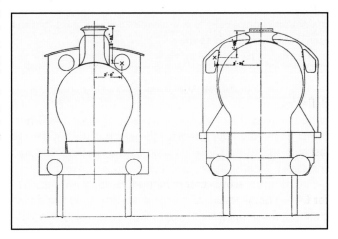

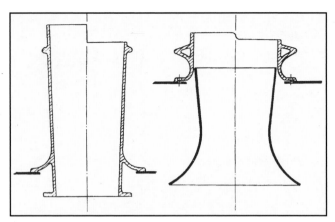

In similar vein, capuchon variations.

Examples of snaps taken at the time of the experiments. Clearly it will be seen that certain types of 'deflector' produced improved results but against this came practicalities in access and maintenance to the engine generally. We may say that the side plates eventually chosen were in effect a best compromise.

The 'Lord Nelson' type vertical deflector plates when fitted to the 'Schools' model were found to direct clean air along the flanks of the boiler and sweep away smoke-contaminated air from the area between the smokebox and the dome, but it was noticeable that this side draught was less effective at greater distances from the front of the engine. Smoke from eddies around the chimney eventually diffused into the side draught, so that the conclusion was that whilst these deflectors were 'definitely advantageous', they were 'only imperfectly satisfactory'.

Various alterations were made to the model's deflectors, but the only improvements arose when the plates were extended forwards or when making them higher. It was acknowledged that there were practical limits to this latter course of action.

The NPL also tried a deflector of their own design. This included a markedly convex smokebox front (about half as pronounced as the bullet noses fitted to GWR Nos 5005 and 6014) and a large scoop which directed the oncoming air vertically upwards in front of the chimney. The scoop stood as high as the chimney and projected forwards to the buffer stocks and the tests showed that it was very effective. Holcroft, however, did not mention it in his review and although the NPL device probably did achieve the requirement that any deflector must fit within the loading gauge and must not obstruct the view from the cab, it is difficult to see how it could be mounted safely whilst still enabling use of the smokebox door for access to clear grits etc. The writer suspects that a major and impractically expensive redesign of the front of the loco would have been needed.

Further, in view of the eddying effect observed around the chimney, some oval cross sections were tried, but with little benefit. The 'Schools' model was also altered to make a sloping top to the smokebox with deflectors that resembled the LNER design fitted to their 10000 (the 'hush-hush' loco). The results from this revealed that the steam/smoke trail did not diverge as much and was 'hardly as wide as the firebox'. The trail remained close to the cab roof, but the view from the cab windows was unobstructed. The best results were obtained from this configuration when there was no projection of the chimney above the smooth slope of the smokebox.

When the 'U' class model was tested, it was found that its taper boiler, Belpaire firebox and taller chimney provided some benefit compared with the 'Schools', although the results of different types of smoke deflecting arrangements was 'much the same'.

Holcroft's conclusion from these tests was that two methods of smoke deflection had been revealed: 'the lifting of the smoke by currents of air directed by suitably situated plates and the other to the confinement of the smoke to a width narrower than the cab windows'. The tests had confirmed the 'beneficial effects' of the side plates and so they were subsequently fitted to 'all the modern passenger and mixed traffic engines on the Southern Railway'. He added that 'it was recognised that the plates as adopted were not a perfect solution, but they gave sufficient relief to the enginemen' and were a satisfactory solution.

Modified plates fitted to 'Lord Nelson' No 860 *Lord Hawke* during the period the engine was fitted with an experimental large boiler. There is no information to indicate whether the change made any difference to smoke lifting.

During the discussion that took place following Holcroft's presentation, some results from the experience of the LNER were presented. These can be summarised as follows: that plates and ducts around the chimney had little effect because they could not handle sufficient volumes of air to make an effect on the steam/smoke exhaust; large side plates could be successful but they were an encumbrance and looked ugly; a wedge shaped front to the cab was beneficial; streamlining was beneficial, especially the Bugatti nose as fitted to the 'A4 class', and the contributor indicated that streamlining was as much about smoke clearance as it was about the reduction of power consumption at high speed.

Mr O. V. S. Bulleid, President of the Institution, who was in the chair also took part in the discussion, and whilst noting that long and high-pitched boilers exacerbated the matter of smoke obscuration, also said that engines of the day 'exhausted their steam at a pressure very little above atmosphere, and, particularly in the case of engines with very big chimneys and multiple jets, there was very little energy left in the steam'.

Bulleid added that he 'did not think it would ever be possible to prevent smoke drifting down onto a cab under all conditions' and he suggested that the problem 'was, in fact, almost insoluble'. Historians will note this statement was made some six months after the first 'Merchant Navy' had entered service.

Subsequent Smoke Deflector Changes

However, back in 1931 the decision was made to fit the 'Schools' with vertical deflectors, similar to those fitted to the 'Lord Nelsons', No 907 being the first in August 1931 according to Bradley (*Locomotives of the Southern Railway Part 1*, RCTS 1975). The 'N15X' class was also equipped with 'Lord Nelson' vertical-type deflectors on conversion from tank locos.

The Maunsell 'Moguls' were equipped with 'angled'-type deflectors from 1933 onwards but even then the experiments were not quite over, for No 1410, alone of the class, received

The image referred in the text as it appeared in the *Southern Railway Magazine* for March–April 1942 – and with apologies for the quality. The caption stated: 'The smoke-bow. This reader's snap-shot illustrates in graphic manner the smoke-bow produced at high speed by the smoke deflectors fitted to SR express engines. The deflector plates on each side of the smokebox are set leaning towards one another so that the converging currents of air are shot upwards in the direction of the chimney, their velocity carrying the exhaust smoke clear of the cab lookouts and often clear of the train itself. Smoke-deflectors came into vogue on the SR engines in 1927, after it had been found that smoke discharged from the very short chimneys of modern locomotives tended to drift along the top of the boiler and beat down upon the cab windows. The picture shows U1 class 3-cylinder 2-6-0 1897 making good time through Chilworth with the Newcastle–Ashford through express while signalman Gatford's boys, Dick and Derek, keep a watchful eye on the photographer.'

additional strips of plate at the top of the normal deflectors, making an extension of about 4 inches. The *Southern Railway Magazine* for March–April 1942 used the phrase 'smoke-bow' (bow' apparently referring to an arc shape) to describe the smoke trail curving high above a speeding train. But, although noting that smoke deflectors had been fitted because 'smoke discharged from the very short chimneys of modern locomotives tended to drift along the top of the boiler and beat down upon the cab windows', there was an additional comment that deflectors had 'come into vogue' on the SR engines in 1927, as though the motivation was one of fashion consciousness just as much as safety.

Turbulence and wind could do funny things to deflector plates that were, for whatever reason, not fully secured, as witness No 787 *Sir Menadeuke* in March 1940. *S. C. Townroe*

Opposite top: **The first of the Bulleid experiments at exhaust dispersing both involving No 783 *Sir Gillemere*. This trial was carried out at the end of 1940 and involved three chimneys: the original plus two others spaced equidistant either side of the original. The idea was not perpetuated, so presumably no real benefit resulted. We are not told of the effect upon smoke deflection or for that matter steaming.**

Opposite bottom: **Shortly after at the start of 1941 No 783 appeared with just two chimneys and as can be seen each of these to slightly different design. Again it was an attempt to disperse the exhaust and so make the engine (and train) less obvious to an enemy plane. (Undertaken in the time of the charismatic Mr Bulleid, one might wonder if the idea came from the fertile brain of the CME or was it another?) Note also the storm sheet on the tender which purpose was to be fitted in the event of a 'red' air raid warning and so prevent any light from the firebox being seen from the air. In practice a sheet such as this made footplate conditions almost intolerable. Returning though to the chimney experiments, the main effect was to cover the engine in soot when it passed through the Micheldever tunnels on test – the blast hitting a century of accumulated soot from a different angle! It was not perpetuated and No 783 *Sir Gillemere* seen here at Eastleigh on 7 January 1941 was restored to conventional condition soon after. *B. W. Anwell***

Presumably following a policy that a partial solution was better than no solution at all, especially one that was modern, fashionable and thereby gained favourable publicity, the general application of a style of smoke deflector to the SR's larger tender engines which was similar to the 'King Arthur' type seemed to have balanced complaints from drivers against a feeling that the problems of poor smoke clearance had no complete solution. Further, and remembering Bulleid's 1941 comment on the reduction in the energy left in the steam as a result of the use of multiple jets, with more of the steam's energy being given to useful work in the cylinders and less towards creating a blast in the chimney, some engineers expected that steam and smoke clearance problems would increase. If the problems did increase when the 'Lord Nelsons' and 'Schools' received multiple-jet blastpipes in the 1938–41 period, then it would appear that little could be done about it without incurring inordinate expense. But for the 'N15s' which received the Bulleid exhaust alterations, there was available the vertical-type deflector to provide a little more relief. Since this work was somewhat sporadically carried out, and on two locos it was not carried out at all, the pressures calling for improvement do not appear to have been significantly greater than the benefits resulting from the effort involved in making changes.

The Bulleid Experience in Outline

For the Maunsell-designed locomotives, that was that, but the next generation of SR locomotives, the Bulleid Pacifics, encountered smoke clearance problems of a different nature and the writer wonders whether the designer was influenced, even misled, by some of the apparently successful findings of the 1931 wind tunnel tests. The 'Schools' model altered with a sloping smokebox top, lack of chimney projection and wrapped-around top casing has some similarity with the 'Merchant Navy' design. Further, some of the findings of the LNER that streamlining aided smoke clearance are followed in Bulleid's approach to the outline of his Pacifics. Did Bulleid expect the 'Merchant Navy' steam and smoke exhaust to be confined into a narrow trail that did not impinge upon the cab windows? Unfortunately, the initial 'Widows Peak' casing front design was not successful and Nos 21C6 and 21C10 received experiments in 1943 that were the first of a number of changes attempting to cure this new smoke clearance nuisance.

Wind tunnel tests carried out at Southampton University using a 'Merchant Navy' model eight feet long, revealed that the original design had insufficient space for air entering the front casing to be released around the chimney and sides of

Drifting smoke on No 21C17 _Belgian Marine_.

'Tacked-on' deflectors on No 21C7 *Aberdeen Commonwealth*, prior to when Wing Commander Cave-Brown began his experiments at Southampton. Around this time wool tufts were added to the front end of at least one member of the class in the way of investigating air-flow as was then standard aircraft practice. Very few conclusions could have been reached from the footplate despite reported efforts with a cine camera. Some brave soul also rode on the front of one engine in operation – perhaps this one – and on a pre-arranged whistle signal let go bags of confetti in the hope of plotting their course!

the smokebox. The oncoming air instead was forced to overflow outwards around the casing in front of the smokebox, causing a 'dead' air layer to build up alongside in a mass that filled with smoke and steam and moved along with the loco. Having established that the wind tunnel configuration accurately reproduced conditions observed in the full-size locomotives, various alternative shapes were tried on the model. The solution was to alter the front casing to provide more space for air flowing around the chimney and to provide new platework, open at the top and rear, that contained the air and directed it along the casing (so clearing much of this 'dead' air) and upwards – and helping the exhaust to lift.

Even then there were frequent conditions when this did not work. Accordingly smoke deflectors were lengthened (mostly during 1947), with the benefit of improving the smoke lift in the vicinity of the cab. Certain locos of those involved in the 1948 exchange trials (Nos 34004, 34005, 34006 and 35020) were given an additional extension to the smoke deflectors to give further benefit at the cab. Although successful, these latter extensions detracted from the appearance of the engine. Separately, No 34039 received a forward extension of its deflectors and when considered in the light of the 1931 findings, this could have been expected to offer an improvement, but no other Pacifics were so treated. Alterations to the fairing behind the chimney, a vent behind the chimney on 34004 and chimneys with and without lips were also tried to gain an improvement, but to the writer's mind, the minimal scale of such changes could not be significant.

Later changes to 34035 and 34049 following the Lewisham accident of 1957 (when signals were missed and where poor smoke clearance was said to have exacerbated foggy atmospheric conditions) seemed to repeat previous work: the reformation of the front casing resembled the unsuccessful 1943 attempts. Only the Giesl ejector fitted to No 34064 in 1962 offered a significant solution (had Bulleid remained in office, one wonders whether this work would have been carried out sooner). Here the velocity of the exhaust through a narrow chimney, relatively free from low pressure zones and eddies, provided better characteristics for smoke clearance. Unfortunately it was too late and 1967 was soon upon us.

So Bulleid was almost exactly right: the problem of smoke clearance was almost insoluble. After the light Pacifics his next design was the 'Leader' and in that, at least. the driver had a good, clear view of where he was leading the whole train!

The writer acknowledges with thanks assistance from the late Tony Sedgwick regarding dates for the first fitting of deflectors recorded by the late George Woodward, and to Eric Youldon for searching out evidence to help clarify certain matters concerning the experimental deflectors, the deflectors fitted to the 'H15' locos and the dates of the alterations to the Urie 'N15' locos following their fitting with multiple jet blastpipes.

An extreme case of smoke drifting although not all might be as it seems at first glance. Here the exhaust pipe from the right-hand cylinder has fractured whilst the engine is in charge of the 1.15pm Cannon Street to Ramsgate. The engine is approaching Grove Park with a cold easterly crosswind and absolutely no view ahead for the fireman when steam was applied. The driver could well have failed the engine with such a defect but he at least was able to maintain a reasonable view. *J. G. Click*

References:

Holcroft, H., 'Smoke deflectors for Locomotives' The Institute of Locomotive Engineers. Vol XXX1 No 164. Nov–Dec 1941.

The presentation and subsequent discussion may be summarised as follows: Includes an abstract of a National Physical Laboratory report by F. C. Johansen on experiments with models of the 'U' and 'V' classes: mainly the latter. Both the paper and the discussion range far beyond the 'U' and 'V' classes and considerable attention is paid both to the successful smoke-lifting propensities of the streamlined 'A4' Pacifics and their precursors, as well as to the height of the chimney (possibly why the GWR did not require smoke deflectors), to the louvres fitted to the Jones locomotives on the Highland Railway, and to the predominant direction of travel (it is argued that strong head winds caused the greatest problem and that is why the London & South Western Section caused greater problems than the Brighton mainline). Holcroft cites both D. K. Clark and Colburn for references to capuchons. Many experimental designs adopted on the SR mainly for the 'King Arthur' class are illustrated. E. Windle (pp. 490-9 described the system adopted for the 'A4' and for the 'P2' class, although it was B. Spencer (p. 503 and 504) who showed how smoke deflection on the 'A4' class was greatly enhanced by modifying the rear of the chimney (earlier a continuous line from the front of the chimney along the boiler casing had been envisaged). Windle also showed that some of the many experimental smokebox/chimney arrangements had been evaluated on the non-streamlined Pacifics. and on the 'P2' 2-8-2s. The connection with the Bugatti railcars in the case of the 'A4' is also mentioned. E. C. Poultney uses the term 'blinkers' and considered that there appeared to be no difference in smoke lifting terms between those fitted with smoke deflectors and the tapered-boiler locomotives. A. R. Ewer (page 499) used the mention of streamlining to condemn it in terms of accessibility. W. A. Willox (pp. 500-1) returned to the topic of chimneys on the GWR and noted that 'recent' Castle class locomotives had shorter chimneys. He also referred to the French Huet system and to the Pottier system which eliminated head wind from the front of the cab. J. Clayton (pp. 501-2) considered that the alignment of the mainlines had some

Practicalities in smoke lifting. No 34003 *Plymouth* has the final development so far as the Bulleid design was concerned: deflector plates set back from the running plate and as much towards 'health and safety' as was applicable at the time, viz handrails and handholds. The 'Terrier' alongside would not need such refinements not just because of the slower speed it would travel but also because of the tall chimney provided. No tank engines in the UK were ever fitted with deflectors although the spark arrestor and pigeon atop No 32650 may be noted!

influence on smoke deflection: on the SR the problem was greatest on the West of England mainline, although this contrasted with the GWR where smoke drifting did not appear to be a problem. D. W. Peacock (pp. 502-3) spoke of wind tunnel work and noted that smoke deflector plates should be placed 'well in front of the smokebox'. O. V. S. Bulleid (pp. 503-4) considered that long boilers accentuated the problem of drifting smoke and suggested that the problem was 'almost insoluble'. Replying to the discussion Holcroft (p. 505) considered that ashpan pressure was a significant factor in blowbacks induced by tunnels, and that closing the dampers removed the risk. F. C. Johansen made a written contribution (507-9) which considered Jones' louvred chimneys on the HR and the increase in air resistance induced by deflector plates.

(We would recommend readers attempt to obtain a copy of the Holcroft paper. It really does make for fascinating reading. Whilst reading John Harvey's article I took the opportunity to order a copy through my local library: £6.00 and approximately one week, money well worth spending – Ed.)

Bradley, D. L., *LSWR Locomotives: the Urie Classes*, Wild Swan, 1987.

Bradley, D. L., *Locomotives of the LSWR Part 2*, RCTS, 1976.

Bradley, D. L., *Locomotives of the Southern Railway, Part 2*, RCTS, 1976.

Bulleid, O. V. S., 'Some notes on the "Merchant Navy" Class Locomotives of the Southern Railway, *Proc. I Mech E*, 1945.

Haresnape, B. *Maunsell Locomotives, A Pictorial History*, Ian Allan, 1977.

Nock, O. S., *The Southern King Arthur Family*, David & Charles, 1976.

Winkworth, D., *The Schools 4-4-0s*, George Allen & Unwin, 1982.

(This article originally appeared with different illustrations in *Southern Notebook* Issues No 153 and 154 in 2001 and 2002. It is reproduced with the kind permission of the Editor of *Southern Notebook* and who is of course also the author of the actual piece.)

(One) Special Train in Colour

On 26 September 1953, the Railway Enthusiasts Club (REC) of Farnborough organised the 'Hants & Surrey Tour', a special train from North Camp to Guildford; thence to Tongham and back to Guildford; from Guildford via Aldershot and Farnham to Bordon – with a trip on the Longmoor Military Railway included behind LMR No 401 – and finally retracing the journey via Ash to Guildford. Motive power for the BR section was the last survivor of the Drummond 'L12' 4-4-0 class No 30434, then based at Guildford.

No 30434's arrival at Tongham created quite a stir as this was reputed to have been the first passenger train – albeit a special – that had visited the station for 16 years. The working was also the first special operated by the REC although they would become prolific in organising and running various trips in later years. (The REC is still in existence and puts on an excellent model show annually in September at Woking although it no longer operates railtours.) The two views show the engine and what was a set of five coaches, including pull-push set No 348, at North Camp, the engine well spruced up for the working.

Two views of No 30434 at North Camp. *Trevor Owen/Hugh Davies*

In July and August of the following year, 1954, No 30434 was employed as carriage pilot at Basingstoke, on one occasion being summonsed to take over from an ailing 'S15' at the head of an up Channel Island express which it successfully worked over the 47¾ miles to Waterloo in 60 minutes, a respectable average of just over 45mph for what was likely a heavy train. This however would be its swansong for No 30434 was finally withdrawn in April 1956 and broken up shortly afterwards although the boiler was considered suitable for stationary use in the Eastleigh erecting shop which continued until June 1959. None of the 20 members of the type was preserved.

An Engine Driver Remembers ...

Brinley G. Prust talking to Marilyn Abbott in May 2009, with grateful thanks to Rod Garner

My name is Brinley George Prust and I was born at Clampits, Fremington, in 1927. I started on the Railway as an engine cleaner at Barnstaple Junction in about 1942. I'd only been on that for about six months when they wanted me to go as a steam raiser, which was promotion. I had to go around the engines at night checking the fires, the boilers and pressures etc. Then a vacancy came up at Torrington as steam raiser. There were two of us down there, me and a chap called Leonard Dubb. We had to look after three engines, all placed at different dispersible points; one in the shed, one in the coal road and one in the cattle dock because of the potential of enemy action – the War was on then and there were no lights. We used to get a blue and a yellow warning and then red if the enemy was overhead. We were still running around with flare lamps as that was the only light we had. One night we had to shovel out 20-ton of coal onto the coal stage and that was a bit rough on us as we weren't very big chaps then.

Some nights, well most nights, there would be some miserable old driver who would tell the fireman to put the fires out, so two engines you could be sure wouldn't have any fire in but the third, which would be the last train arriving at Torrington at three minutes past nine, would have. When the crew had gone home we would stoke the fire up a bit on the main engine and when this was burning well we would shovel some of the fire out and take it over to the other engines and chuck it into the firebox. Luckily we had a big scoop and a wheelbarrow (we would also wet the floorboards of the cab first), throwing the burning coal in the fire box on top of some previously cut sleepers. We used to have to chop up about three to five sleepers a week into something like two-foot lengths, sawing them first with a saw with bare teeth, then split them in two about two inches square and put them,

Barnstaple Junction shed in July 1956. 'N' class No 31836 is outside the front of the two-road shed which stood to the left of the main station.

'M7' No 30251 at Torrington with the 4.38pm train to Barnstaple in August 1959.

usually wet, in the smoke box of the last engine to come in so that it was hot. One night we did all of this work, got the three engines lit up, got the coal in, filled up the bunkers on the coal stage and made sure the boilers were all right and went to make a cup of tea. When we came back one of the main supporting wooden beams across the engine shed was burning! We had to get the high-pressure hose pipe, which was made of leather with studs down it and a long copper nozzle, which would shoot water about 30 feet – it was as heavy as heck – and go to the fire hydrant and turn it on. We put the fire out and nobody ever noticed. What had happened was we had stopped an engine with the chimney under the wooden beam. We should have known better, well we did know but had forgotten as engines were supposed to be stabled between the crossbeams, so leaving about seven or eight feet before you hit the roof, especially if the blower was turned on [and] a few sparks went up the chimney. We could have caught the whole place alight.

There was another incident, a similar thing. We were bringing an engine in off the pit which was outside as we wanted to throw the clinker and ashes from the ash pan out of that pit and on to the side to be able to load them on to a truck in the coal road. Anyway, we decided to get the engine into the shed and took off the hand brake. We only had about 10 pound of vacuum brake and there wasn't any power in that. It was also slightly downhill to the shed. We started the engine moving and couldn't stop it. It hit the stop blocks and then went up against the fireplace in the restroom or cabin as we called it and cracked all the bricks inside. It's a wonder we escaped unharmed from all this.

Did many railwaymen leave to join the forces when the War started? Yes, some of the railway blokes who had just started firing did, as they thought there must be something better as firing was hard work. You could be working all hours of the day or night. On duty at 2.00am, midnight or 8.00am, the same sort of shifts as miners. It was then realised that there weren't enough firemen to keep the trains going so we juniors had rapid promotion. We were taken half-trained and put on the

job. Usually you started off on branch lines like Barnstaple to Ilfracombe, Barnstaple to Torrington, or Torrington out to Halwill Junction and back, although sometimes there just wouldn't be anyone to cover the main line work and you had to. We would hope and pray that some fireman wouldn't turn up so we could go on the main line from Barnstaple to Exeter but when you did you wish you hadn't. That was hard work. We had the old engines, some falling to pieces before the war started. A lot of old 'N' classes built at Woolwich Arsenal after World War 1. My father was a fireman at Nine Elms and he had these engines first and then they came down this end. They ought to have been scrapped before I started. Later the 'West Country' class came and that was a darn good engine, no matter what these amateurs called them. People would call them 'spam cans' and all sorts of rude words. They would do the job and also had a rocking grate and if the fire wasn't so good there was a big lever which opened up a catch and you would work the fire bars and let the clinker through and allow air in so the fire would keep going. You could also put the fire to one side, scoop the ash etc into the middle, drop the grate, open up another catch, put the lever on and open the grate so it dropped down in the ash pan. With the ash pan flapper doors already open it all went straight down into the pit so there was no need to use a shovel, only for putting it to one side. When you had done one side you would put the clinker over to the other side and pile a load of coal on, put the blower on a bit, then shovel the rest down. You then went to the side of the engine – you didn't have to go under it to close the ash pan when you had finished. In the old engines you had to get underneath and rake it out. It was like a flour mill, it would all come down and you would get plastered with ashes, dust and dirt especially if the wind was blowing your way but you had no choice, sometimes you had to rake the back of the box and the ash pan. It was a heck of a job to get it out. Most engines had water cocks in the ash pan but very few worked. The wet ash used to block them up. It was a poor system but I don't know what else could have been done. Then the Government decided they would make the railway a reserved occupation.

No 34078 *222 Squadron* at Ilfracombe
with the 12.15pm to Waterloo,
6 September 1963.

In the meantime I had joined the Sea Scouts and was getting on well. There were

half a dozen or so others who did the same. We had some good teachers, retired from Dartmouth Naval College, and they knew their stuff. I then volunteered for the Navy, got accepted and went to Bristol, wearing Sea Cadet uniform. The first day we had an eye test, the second day a medical followed by intelligence tests and so on. On the last day we had trigonometry and algebra, something I had never done as I had only gone to a village school. There were about 20 who had to do this, with only two or three who had attended Grammar school and learnt it. They passed the tests. I couldn't even start. As the rest of us were waiting, a CPO (about six foot two and two foot six wide) came up to me and asked what the matter was. When I told him I couldn't do it he told me to pack my kit bag and follow him as the Commanding Officer wanted to see me. I wondered what I had done. The CO asked if I wanted the good news, or the bad news first? I said the good and he informed me that I had passed to go as a stoker in the Royal Navy. I had forgotten to mention to him that the Railway would not release me unless I went to an equivalent rank to that which I was already holding. As I had just been made up to fireman that meant as a stoker in the Navy except they didn't have many coal burning ships left! It was all oil-fired but I already knew the basic principles. I thanked the CO and waited for the bad news. This was that the Railway would be keeping me and that I had to report to the shed master in Barnstaple on Monday morning at 8.00am. Obviously the Navy had been in touch with the Railway, or was it the other way around?

By this time it was 5.00pm on Friday night and I was given my discharge papers and a pass and was driven by a rating to Bristol Temple Meads station. I arrived at Exeter St David's to see the last train disappearing down the tracks. I spent the night in the station, a horrible, cold place but I wasn't the only one. There were WAAFs, soldiers, sailors, in fact all sorts. In the morning about 4.00am I walked across to platform three, the

one for Barnstaple, just as a train was coming in, either the mail or paper train. Fortunately I had been fireman to the driver in the past and he was happy to give me a lift on the footplate. Once in Barnstaple I got a lift back to Bickington with the driver of a Mother's Pride van who knew me. I knew my parents would be up as Dad was a farm bailiff and had to be at work by 7.30. On Monday morning I reported for work and resumed the duties I had before I went to Bristol. I worked from the Junction to Ilfracombe, over the iron bridge to the Town station, and over the swing bridge to Pottington which opened up to let vessels go up the River Yeo. To open and close that bridge there was a kind of capstan arrangement with blokes running around like they did on the old ships. The token was given up at Pottington, then on to Duckpool (Chivenor) and to Wrafton.

I remember one evening I was on the 5.15am on my way to Ilfracombe for relief work. The driver was Frank Cox – this was before he was appointed Shed Master at the junction – the fireman was 'Titch' Hill. Along the way a man jumped out of the bushes and went under the wheels. Titch saw this and immediately went to Frank pushing and prodding him as he couldn't get the words out due to the shock. By the time he had recovered enough to say what had happened the train was at Wrafton where the tragic incident was reported. Another time I was with a driver called Bert Johns and we were coming out of the goods yard at Braunton where there was a ground frame (Braunton Gates near Score Farm) with levers which controlled the entry and exit to the yard and also the crossing gates. We had to reverse out unable to see anything, unfortunately just as an old lady came through the kissing gates at the crossing and was run over. Perhaps she did not see us.

Other unpleasantries recalled from this time were truck loads of bones crawling with maggots destined for the Braunton glue factory. There was a track leading either into the goods shed or just beside it and we would put four or five loads of stinking bones there, whacking great cow bones they were. No one ever needed to ask where Braunton was, they could smell

Braunton signal box, September 1963. The signal box here was at the north end of the site. Braunton Gates, referred to in the text, was at the south end of the station, 10 chains (220 yards) closer to Barnstaple.

it. Other times when the local sewerage works were cleaned out, we would have six or eight trucks of 'black stuff' which would go to the Bulb Farm. I spent a lot of time in Braunton yard shunting, often on relief to cover the Ilfracombe firemen when they took their annual leave. I remember there was Reg Ackland and other chaps called Bill Bray, Ernie Thorne and Bert Johns.

I recall the situation if I was booked to work the 2.00pm from Ilfracombe. I would leave home, I am guessing at about noon, make my way to Barnstaple shed and put my bike along with the driver's on the tender. When we arrived with the engine at Ilfracombe, there would be some shunting to do to make up the train and then it was off up the bank to Exeter. We would leave Exeter again on the last train to Ilfracombe, but this was where the engine would now be put away. The bus depot was about a mile away and it was impossible to make it in time for the last bus so we collected our bikes from the shed where they had been left and went part of the way down to the town where we would go through a little narrow gap with a bar rail down the middle – it is still there to this day. Ilfracombe station was high above the town and the path down was steep: about one in three or one in four. We would ride all the way to Mullacott Cross, then downhill to Braunton. If the wind was blowing towards Barnstaple it was a great help. If it was against you it could be agony especially if it was also raining and freezing cold. No one would do it today. I remember Dad saying when he came home after the War and was doing relief work he would cycle to Umberleigh from Braunton!

One night I was cycling back from Ilfracombe with a chap called Frank who had a box on the back of his bike. He kept all sorts in it; worsted wool for the trimmings to suck oil from one oil box to another and some copper all twisted up and made as plug trimmings to put in the big end. The big end would throw the oil up and then it would only allow so much to go down at a time. There were corks with canes in to let in the air. If the gauge glass broke, and they did sometimes, you had to replace them yourself so Frank would have a couple of spare ones and of course a spanner and even clothes pegs, they were handy for all sorts of jobs. He had everything in that box. Anyway this particular night we had just passed where

Mullacott Cross is. There must have been a pot hole that he missed as the strap broke, the box jumped off and flew open and everything went all over the road. We only had a hand torch as lights weren't allowed in the War. We were on the ground for about half an hour looking for all the bits and pieces and we only found about half of it as a lot went into the hedge.

Some nights if it was blowing a gale we could hardly get the train past Mortehoe. We could have been on the engine all day and despite the fire it would be freezing, it was awful. One of my worse trips was one Christmas Eve with a special from Exeter. We were late leaving Barnstaple, I remember the driver, a chap called Dyer Neale, nicknamed 'Whisper' and who kept quoting (Clement Clarke Moore's '1823') 'Twas the Night before Christmas'. The further we went the worse the weather got. At Willingcott we ran out of steam and stopped under the bridge. It took twenty minutes to get the pressure back but we eventually got to Mortehoe and then down to Ilfracombe. The passengers weren't too pleased about the delay and neither were those waiting on Ilfracombe station in the freezing cold for the train to arrive.

Can you remember what year the Railway became a reserved occupation? I think it was about 1942 when I went to Bristol for interview with the Navy. When you were on the Railway at that time you were issued with an oval-shaped badge, brass with a blue background and the profile of an engine on the top which said 'Railway Service'. On the back was a number so that if you got blown up or anything and the badge was found the authorities would know who you were – and that you had 'had it'! Once we had been issued with a badge (which we wore all the time) it wasn't so bad, as before if you went in a pub where there were Americans they would heave you out as they thought you were a conscientious objector or suchlike. On Saturday nights, when I was on the Torrington line, we would go down on the 6.30pm, then walk up to the town for a drink. There was one pub, the Setting Sun, in the middle they had one of those tortoise stoves, the pipe went up the middle with a bar. There were iron rails around. It used to get that crowded blokes would get their hands singed! I remember one night we were in there when beer was on

The climb to the summit on the Ilfracombe line was a trial in either direction, as witness here with this Bulleid 'steam on and sanders working'. *George Heiron*

ration. There was one barrel and when that was gone that was it. The Americans came in and wanted whisky (they didn't go much on beer) and if they couldn't get it they would get real ratty. They would storm behind the bar and look for themselves, it was a bit scary but they didn't care. Once they had gone, the landlord would close the door and manage to squeeze some beer from the empty barrel. What we did find is that when we went into a pub where there were Americans who had already had a few drinks they would grab you by the scruff of the neck and sling you out. Huge fellas they were. The funny thing was though that once I got sent to 'Combe, where there were again a lot of Americans, it was very different, as they didn't bother us.

I was up and down to Ilfracombe a lot. We used to leave from the Town station at Barnstaple with a train called the boozer train at 10.30. There was a big man there called Squires

who was in charge of letting everyone on to the platform. We are talking about a train of perhaps four coaches which would hold more or less three hundred people, but five hundred or so would want to get on. These were ATS girls, Air Force girls, Americans, but not many of our chaps as they were away. On the way to Wrafton and Braunton, some would take great delight in pulling the communication cord on what were non-corridor trains. Each time this happened the guard would walk along the outside of the train and shine his oil lamp, find the coach with a red tab sticking out which meant the cord had been pulled and that had opened the air valve and put the brakes on. Sometimes the train would be stopped three times in half an hour as they were all so boozed up. There were so many of them they couldn't be stopped jumping on the train as it was always such a mad rush. It got so bad, a couple of American 'Snowdrops' (Military Police) were put on duty, which helped a bit but even so, there would be perhaps a hundred on the train who had tickets and say, three hundred who didn't. After stopping the train umpteen times getting to Braunton the men wouldn't get out on the platform side, instead they would open the door on the other side, jump out, cross the track on to the opposite platform, get into the goods yard and scatter everywhere. This went on for weeks.

In the end I don't know who organised it but one particular night they jumped out and went across the goods yard and found waiting for them about 20 or 30 Military Police waiting for them. The GIs didn't argue with them. The MPs used to carry large truncheon like sticks to clobber them and then put them in wagons and took them off to camp. They never did it again. I've got an idea that some of the guards would lock the carriage doors before the train left Town station. Of course they weren't supposed to do this but it did stop anyone getting out the wrong side.

I remember one night, we got to Town station and two Americans came up and greeted me saying they were on the railroad back in the States and asked if they could ride on the footplate. I said 'no' as they were boozed up. Sid, the driver was a bit worried and picked up the coal pick starting to wave it at them. They took the hint and disappeared and at the time we never saw where it was they went, although we did find out later.

There was a strong wind blowing up the river towards Town station together with driving rain. We also had a tender full of dusty coal, more slack than anything else. It transpired they had gone up to the back of the tender by the water filler, not a very big space. Of course there they were getting all the spray from this filthy coal dust plus the benefit of the rain. When they climbed down at Braunton they looked like a couple of scarecrows, as black as rooks. Looking as they did, they were arrested and locked up with no hesitation.

In 1947, the winter with the heavy snow, we had come from Exeter to Ilfracombe. Because of the weather we weren't able to ride the bikes home so we took the cushions out of one of the coaches and put them in the packers hut. We had taken

steps 'insurance' to know where the key was hidden. We stoked the fire up and it was quite cosy. About 2.00am I was woken up and heard an engine whistling and wondered what was up. Looking out I also saw that the signal box was open. Unbeknown to us, an engine had been organised to run between Barnstaple and Ilfracombe to keep the line open. I made my way across to see who the driver was, the snow being past my knees by this time, but I made it to the shed. I knew the crew so we damped the fire in the hut, locked up, put the cushions back and climbed on the footplate, heading off towards Barnstaple: We got as far as where the bridge goes over to Lee in the very steep-sided and rocky cutting where the nearby fields are about 15 feet above the railway. There was a terrific wind blowing all the snow down from the fields into the cutting and completely burying the track we were on, although it wasn't so bad on the down line. We went around a bend and smack, everything on the engine went flying, tea cans, oil cans everything. Both my driver and me ended up by the hand brake. It was lucky we weren't smashed to pieces but none of us was hurt. Looking over the side the snow was level with the footplate, six or seven feet above the ground.

There were rules to carry out in this situation, the fireman had to go down the steps on the downside of the track and walk to Mortehoe. He was a tall chap but he almost disappeared in the snow. We waited and waited but he never returned. We were getting cold as we'd put the fire out as there was no idea how long we might be stuck but soon wished that we hadn't. After about half an hour we heard a whistle; a train with about 20 trucks attached, carrying 20 or 30 packers and their shovels stopped opposite us. They proceeded to dig us out filling up about seven trucks with snow in about an hour. We of course couldn't move. Their train was then allowed to go through to Ilfracombe where it left the trucks to wait for the snow to melt. The engine then returned and pushed us back to Barnstaple. It must have been about 7.00 or 8.00 in the morning by the time we got home. Our fireman, 'Papa' Parr who had walked to the signal box was,

Double heading at Barnstaple Town. Southern 'N' class 2-6-0 No 31847 and GWR 2-6-0 No 6343 with the 10.12 SO service from Ilfracombe to Taunton, 18 July 1956.

according to the rules, supposed to return after the correct procedure was followed and he had signed the book informing the signalman the position of the train. However by the time he'd struggled to Mortehoe he had had enough and decided to stay put and instead was picked up by us on our way through. It all worked out happily ever after but was an experience we would never forget.

As a fireman, you went to work every day and did the same job for a week: you might have the same engine for a week but every day was different, every day you would pick up that engine and go somewhere and it would be different. If it was raining drizzly rain, under trees going up a climb it would be different. When we went to Torrington we would go through the woods and the leaves would fall thick and heavy on the track and be squashed. There was chlorophyll and all sorts in those leaves. We would manage three of four revolutions and the wheels would come to a stop even though we were using the sanders. In later years I was on the Ilfracombe line when DMUs and the 'D63xx' type were running. They were horrible things but had one advantage over steam as you could sit down in reasonable comfort. Also your back wasn't freezing and your knees weren't burning. When you opened the firebox door going up to Mortehoe your knees could start singeing. The DMUs were like having bus engines underneath, two in the front and two in the back. They were difficult to start off with but we got to know what the faults were and what to do about them so it wasn't too bad. They were comfortable, and they had cab heaters and windscreen wipers. Funny old things though as they rocked and rolled all the time. Not the best of rides, however, but they did the job, a bit like having two buses joined together. Then the '7000' ('Hymek') class was brought in, they were good engines.

From Ilfracombe it was a dead start, 1 in 36. If it was a nice day they wouldn't slip too much and you could get out with a

No 34002 *Salisbury* (at Ilfracombe) and no doubt contemplating the steep climb which commences immediately at the end of the platform on the way to Barnstaple, Exeter and beyond. *George Heiron*

bigger load than with a steam engine would take, no bother. When you got to the tunnel after leaving Ilfracombe it would be dripping with water which was inclined to make steam engine wheels slip. One slip in that tunnel at 20mph and you could come to a standstill even before you could shut the regulator to counteract it. I would always put the sand on once I got in the tunnel to try and prevent that if I had a heavy load on. The idea was that prevention was better than cure. If you were only doing 5mph you would stop before you could gain control of it. If the engine did slip, by the time you shut the regulator and exhausted the steam, the wheels were spinning and that didn't do the engine much good.

What year did you become a driver? It was 1952, but 1960 when I became a full-blown registered driver. Before that, you were passed for driving but still had to do firing jobs if required. You had to get 360 driving turns before you got to first rate driver pay and another 363 before second rate. I did a lot of driving from 1951 onwards and managed 10 years before we were all made redundant in 1970, when the Barnstaple to Ilfracombe line was closed. Before that, I had got a driver's job on the Torrington line and when that depot closed I went back to Barnstaple and ended up going to Ilfracombe, Exeter and Taunton again.

The Torrington line was a lovely job. Jack Brock was the lengthman between Petrockstowe and Torrington. We would ask him, if we put a spare truck on for a Sunday, could we have 20 bundles of bean sticks and we knew that they would he waiting in the hut, all tied up ready. We would give some to anyone else who wanted them and take the rest back to Fremington where I lived then. The signalman there, a chap called Bill Hill, would load them onto a long station barrow and take them to my garden. We would always help each other out. I remember once Jack wanted some coal thrown out half way to Yarde Down cottages. We had about six empty trucks and a guard's van which wasn't stopping us at all. We scampered up there at 20mph and I had a great big lump that had come down from the bunker which I put ready to one side. We came round the bend passed Bagbere and I got ready with the piece. I could just about lift it, and rested it on the handrail. When we got about twenty yards from the hut I chucked it out. It landed on this mossy hank and bounced and spun around and bounced and bounced again then it went 'Bang' right through the shed door. I don't know what happened to it after that, t'was like Barnes Wallis' bouncing bomb! Jack said later, 'When I asked for a lump of coal I didn't want the so and so put in the fireplace'.

Did you drive the 'Devon Belle'? I was involved but only as a fireman. It was about 500 tons and had the fastest booked time from Ilfracombe to Exeter – 55 minutes I think it was. You really had to go with that train. We were supposed to come down to about 5 or 10mph to change the token but we went through about twice that speed. You had to keep your timing right as it was a difficult train. It left 'Combe with about five and a half thousand gallons of water and would have nothing left by the time it reached Exeter St David's. I wasn't sorry to see it go, although it was a nice train for the passengers and very

comfortable but the heaviest train they used to bring out. It also had to have an engine on the back from Braunton (as did many of the long trains carrying holiday makers in the summer) to push it up to Mortehoe. In the other direction it needed a push from Ilfracombe to Morte' as well. If you had stopped in the tunnel without an engine on the back the carriages maybe would shunt slightly back and forward because of the springs. That could lead to the couplings snapping and goodness knows what would happen then. The driver would murder the engine, catching the cornfields and everything else alight. I remember now, talking about it, the packers were about a quarter of a mile Barnstaple side of Heanton Court. They had been there about week building a lovely shed, one of the modern ones with two-inch sleeper boarding, with windows and a nice fireplace. They had just about finished and we came down with the 'Devon Belle'. I have forgotten who the driver was. I think he went to nick her up a bit and made a bit of a mistake. Instead the power of the engine took over and slammed her right down in full gear so it was chucking lumps of burning coal out of the chimney. He put it right in a matter of seconds but it was too late. We went through to Ilfracombe and when we returned all that was left of that shed were the four corner posts, the rest was still smoking. Another day at Wrafton, same engine, same train, we were leaving the station passing the cornfield by the station house. The corn was ready to cut but they didn't need to bother as the driver caught it alight and did the job for them. No one liked driving the 'Devon Belle' much. A couple of firemen even packed it in, they couldn't keep up with the fire. We were relieved when it finished. I don't think it was paying much anyway.

I did spend many a happy hour though catching trout in the River Caen in Braunton whilst waiting to bank the 'Devon Belle'. There was an old lady who always sat by an upstairs window in Score Farm that we waved to.

Later on, the system was altered and we could come back from Ilfracombe at the end of our shift on a light engine. One night we got to Braunton and were told we couldn't go on as usual as the signalman wasn't getting any response from Velator crossing. However he later allowed us to proceed under caution. We got to the crossing, the light was red and the gate still across in front of us. I went over to Taffy Wilkins (a guard who lived nearby) and he came back and opened the gates and pulled the signal to let us go. Just as we were about to leave, a bloke came round the corner, peddling like mad on his bike. It was the crossing keeper who had forgotten all about us coming back on the light engine!

I remember a driver on the Mail train from Exeter coming round the corner by Heanton Court. It was blowing a gale. He somehow managed to miss the signal for Duckpool (Chivenor) and went right through the gates. He got a written warning and there was an inquiry as to how it happened. On the Bulleid engines the driver is on the left-hand side and the fireman on the right and he should have seen the signal on the right and warned the driver that the signal was red. The gates were renewed and then unbelievably about a fortnight later the same bloke went through them again. He was taken off the footplate then.

No 34068 *Kenley* **arriving at Exeter St Davids from Ilfracombe with the up 2.55pm train, 9 September 1961.**

Another thought. We used to leave with a goods train from Barnstaple going to 'Combe and with tankers on the back. No one ever thought anything of them and we put them off in the back of Wrafton goods yard behind the signal box on the siding nearest to the aerodrome. There were also some sealed wagons, no one could see what was in them but I am sure they contained ammo for the aircraft. We found out afterwards that the tankers had aviation fuel in them. Nothing was marked explosive or flammable then. I reckon there was more that went in and out of Wrafton station than we ever knew about and they certainly were not going to tell drivers and firemen there were bombs or high explosives on the back of our engines.

I have vague memories of being told that a train was hit during the War? I can tell you about that. It was about 1940/41 and the engine was No 1842. It got machine gunned along by Ashford Strand, near Heanton Court. Bert Johns was the driver, I can't remember who the fireman was. The engine ran for a long time afterwards with the bullet holes in the casing. Fortunately they didn't go through the boiler: I can see the holes now, on the right-hand side of the engine.

On the whole did you enjoy your time on the railway and which did you prefer, steam or diesel? Oh yes, I would go back tomorrow if I could. It is difficult to say which I preferred, as steam and diesel were so very different but I would go back to either. My wife agrees that I have never been the same man since I left.

Hatherleigh station on the North Devon & Cornwall Junction Light Railway between Torrington and Halwill Junction. The view was taken on 28 July 1925, one day after formal opening. *Corbis Images*

Woking and Guildford

Peter Tatlow

The overnight goods train from the west often paused at Woking early each morning to allow the heavy commuter traffic for London to pass through. Here 4-6-0 'S15' class No 30839, built at Eastleigh in May 1936, with a bogie flat-sided tender waits to regain the road on its way to Feltham yard on 3 July 1958. The engine survived until September 1965.

The first section of the London to Southampton Railway opened from Nine Elms to Woking on 21 May 1838 and in due course was extended until Southampton was reached two years later. The station was situated about two miles from the existing community of Woking, now known as Old Woking. The present-day Woking developed around the railway, which may account for its High Street having shops only one side and a retaining wall supporting the railway on the other! Nonetheless, as a railway centre, Woking increased in importance as the main line was extended beyond Southampton to Weymouth; the West

of England line branched off from Basingstoke to reach Exeter, Plymouth and beyond. A branch from Woking to Guildford opened on 21 May 1845 and in due course was extended to Portsmouth.

In preparation for the implementation of the Portsmouth and Alton electrification scheme, from 1935 the Southern Railway rebuilt Woking station with four through platforms long enough for 12-car trains, together with shorter bays on the up and down sides. As part of the scheme, the area was re-signalled with three manual boxes being replaced by one power box and three- and four-aspect signals installed; while an Electrical Control building was constructed at the country end of the down-side yard.

At the outset of World War 2, the District Engineer (London West) Office was relocated from Clapham Junction to Woking on

The crack 1.0pm express from Waterloo for the West of England main line heads through Woking on 24 April 1959 hauled by Bulleid 'Merchant Navy' class No 35004 *Cunard White Star* with the first four BR Mark 1 coaches still in carmine and cream livery. The locomotive was out-shopped from Eastleigh in October 1941, rebuilt in July 1958 and withdrawn in October 1965.

the up side at the London end, to be joined by the District Operating staff and the Control Office. The up-side yard at the country end was enlarged and used by the Engineer's Department as a permanent way depot for the pre-assembly of track.

With divisionalisation of the Operating Department, except for the Control Room, their staff moved to Wimbledon. The Bournemouth electrification scheme of 1967 brought to an end steam working not only through Woking, but on the Southern Region as a whole. Reorganisation of the Engineer's Department into divisions in July 1967, led to its staff also moving to Wimbledon or one of the Area Offices.

Extensions of the Guildford line to Godalming and Farnham were authorised in 1846 and opened on 1 October 1849. Nonetheless, from 20 August that year the Reading, Guildford

& Reigate Railway's route (South Eastern & Chatham Railway [SE&CR] from 1852) used the London & South Western Railway's [LSWR] line from Shalford Junction, south of the two tunnels, through Guildford station and to the north along the LSWR tracks as far as Ash Junction. The Portsmouth Direct line from Godalming to Havant was opened on 24 January 1859. From 2 October 1865, the London, Brighton & South Coast Railway's (LBSCR) branch from Horsham joined a little further south at Peasmarsh Junction and the LSWR's own New Guildford came in from the north east on 2 February 1885. Thus, all three of the eventual constituents of the Southern Railway were represented at Guildford until the closure of the Horsham line on 12 June 1965, just as the town of Cranleigh was being developed.

A 2BIL electric multiple unit set from Alton, having just coupled up to the portion from Portsmouth & Southsea, known as the 'Pompey slow', accelerates away from Woking on the local line heading for the metropolis, as it is passed by 'Lord Nelson' class No 30857 *Lord Howe* on the through line with an Up boat train from Southampton Docks, 28 April 1959. No 30857 was completed at Eastleigh in December 1928 and withdrawn in September 1962.

In the up side loop lines to the west of the station, 4-6-0 No 30837 waits with a long down goods train in July 1959. This was a Maunsell version of the 'S15' class built at Eastleigh in January 1928 with a six-wheel flat-sided tender and withdrawn in September 1965. According to the headcode carried, this train originated on the South Eastern Division, presumably having come from either Hither Green or Norwood Junction, and travelled via Clapham Junction, Brentford and Chertsey heading for Basingstoke and either Southampton or Salisbury.

A fine study of 'West Country' class No 34047 *Callington*, made at Brighton Works in November 1946, rebuilt in November 1958 and withdrawn June 1967. Having called at Woking station, it sets off on the final leg of its journey to Waterloo in March 1967 with a train from Bournemouth.

With a morning Salisbury commuter working having called at Woking, modified 'West Country' class No 34108 struggles to get its train on the move again on 28 April 1967. One time named 'Wincanton', a product of Brighton in May 1950 and rebuilt 11 years later, it is now nameless being withdrawn in June 1967. The first two coaches of this semi-fast train are BR compartment stock.

Guildford's cramped motive power depot was located at the south end of the station between the Farnham Road overbridge and the tunnel mouth. Electrification first reached Guildford via the New Guildford line in July 1925. The above-mentioned Portsmouth and Alton scheme brought the third rail through on the main line and round from Aldershot in 1937 with, at the time, partial colour-light re-signalling.

References

BR, Southern Region, Locomotives, Western Section, Diagram book.

Dendy Marshall C. F., *A History of the Southern Railway*, The Southern Railway, 1936, pp 81, 113, 139-140, 170, 299.

Moody G. T., *Southern Electric*, Ian Allan, 1957, pp 25, 64.

Sectional Appendix to WTT, Southern Region, Western Section, BR, 1 Oct 1960, pp120-124.

Sillince D., 'The Horsham & Guildford Direct', *Railway Magazine*, 1966, p127.

Tilling, W. G., *The Locomotives of the Southern Railway (Western Section)*, 1943.

Townroe, S. C., *The Arthurs, Nelsons and Schools of the Southern*, Ian Allan, 1973, p100.

http://www.semgonline.com/steam

On 24 May 1959, ex-LSWR 4-4-0 Drummond 'T9' class, No 30732, departs from Guildford with the 8.10am train for Reading South. No 30732 with a narrow cab and bogie tender was constructed by Messrs Dübs Glasgow in January 1900, superheated in March 1927 and withdrawn in October 1959.

A few days later, the same train was in the hands of No 33016, one of Bulleid's 0-6-0 'Q1' class, known to some as 'Coffee Pots'. Built at Brighton in November 1942, it lasted until August 1963.

Guildford depot was long the home of a short wheelbase tank engine, such as 0-4-0ST 'Ironside' (5ft 6in wheelbase) and 'B4s' (7ft 0in wheelbase), and finally 0-6-0T USA Tanks (10ft 0in wheelbase), to access remote corners of the shed. No 30072 was built by Vulcan Ironworks in 1943 for the US Army Transportation Corps and purchased by the SR in 1946, entering service in April 1947. It lasted until the end of steam on the Southern in July 1967 and is now preserved. Here it is sandwiched between vans as it stands in a siding at the country end of Platform 2 in October 1966. *All photographs by the author*

Southern Railway Traffic Officers Conference
Compiled by David Monk-Steel

Minutes of a meeting held at Waterloo station,
Monday 26 May 1924.
Chaired by Sir Herbert A. Walker KCB.

Views of goods yard are invariably scare, but here is an undated image of Herne Bay. Traffic received appears to consist primarily of bricks.
David Vaughan collection

Fatal Accident to Servant of the Company, Dyke Junction
27 March 1924

At approximately 8.7am a Ganger and two Undermen were working on the line renewing timbers in the down line at Dyke Junction when the Ganger informed the Undermen he required to collect a shovel from the Platelayer's hut. As he walked to the hut he observed the 7.18am Bognor to Victoria train approaching on the up line and also the 8.0am Brighton to Horsham on the down line. He blew his whistle and shouted to the Undermen, but only one of them heard and stepped clear, the other remained in the four-foot of the Up line and was struck by the Bognor train, and was killed. At the inquest a verdict of Accidental Death was returned.

This page and opposite: **Three views of the Dover Harbour Board lines in Southern days. First we see 'P' class 0-6-0 No 555 with a train of tank wagons and clearly of interest to the nearby children. Next a Southern 'O1' No 1108 built in 1897 and which spend much of its time at Dover until withdrawn in 1951. Finally there is a 'close encounter' of what is likely No 1108 again and a Dover Corporation tram.** *All David Vaughan collection*

Sevenoaks 28 March 1924

The signalman prematurely operated No 41 lever controlling the catch points in the Long Siding whilst the empty coaching stock for the 8.25pm Sevenoaks to Tonbridge Empty Train, consisting of seven vehicles, was being shunted into the Down Bay platform before all the vehicles were clear. The wheels of the sixth and seventh vehicles were derailed. There was considerable damage to the permanent way and signalling equipment.

Dover Marine 31 March 1924

At 11.15am engine No 672 was placed on No 4 line prior to proceeding through No 23 points on to the rear of the 9.40am Victoria to Dover Marine arrival in Platform 5. The signalman at Dover Pier 'A' cabin then accepted the 7.30am arrival from Holborn and cleared No 17 lever that operated the route indicator to No 4 line and lowered No 9 home signal. He then realised he had cleared the route on to the line on which the light engine was standing. He attempted to attract the attention of the drivers of both engines and the light engine driver managed to put on steam, and the approaching engine commenced braking, but it was insufficient to avoid a minor collision. The joint inquiry concluded that the signalman was at fault for –

(a) Failing to replace 22 points leading to No 4 line after light engine 672 had sent to stand thereon;

(b) Pulling off the route indicator for No 4 line instead of No 3 and lowering the home signal;

(c) Omitting to place a lever collar on No 17 lever controlling the route indicator to No 4 line.

They also criticised the driver of engine No 672 for failing to carry out Rule 55 clause (b) by not sending his fireman to the signal box to remind the signalman of the presence of the engine. New instructions have been issued prohibiting standing engines in front of the station.

Kew Bridge 31 March 1924

At 6.18pm after the arrival of the 5.40pm electric train from Broad Street the motorman was given a hand signal by the guard to proceed empty into the third road irregularly against the signal. After proceeding about four coach lengths the driver observed the stock for the 6.20pm Kew to Broad Street in the siding, about to depart for the up platform correctly signalled. The Southern Company's signalman observing this irregularity immediately placed the signals to danger against the stock for the 6.20pm and exhibited a red flag. The motorman of the 5.40pm train, seeing this flag then reversed his train, splitting the points which he had previously 'run through' and derailing the fifth vehicle. The responsibility for the derailment rests with LM&S staff who have been suitably dealt with.

Upper Sydenham Tunnel 8 April 1924

At 11.20am during unloading of ballast a hopper wagon of the 10.54am ballast train from Crystal Palace High Level became derailed on high ballast. Control of the unloading movement was hampered by smoke accumulating in the tunnel.

Guildford 12 April 1924

The engine of the 8.15pm Waterloo to Guildford train was derailed on catch points whilst being shunted back along the Cobham line to reach the turntable. The driver misread the ground signal for the down sidings as that for the crossover road.

Glynde 18 April 1924

At 4.7pm the signalman inadvertently operated No 8 (up line to up sidings west) instead of No 7 points up line to up sidings east) lever just as a draft of wagons of the 11.15pm Eastbourne to Lewes goods train was being shunted over them The engine was propelling nine wagons along the up line before attaching them to the train in the siding at the eastern end of the station. Two wagons were derailed.

Plymouth North Road 2 May 1924

At 6.26am the 6.15am passenger train from Friary collided with the rear of the 9.15pm Cardiff to Plymouth parcels train in No 2 platform. The collision was due to the GWR signalman at North Road East signal box lowering the down home signal for No 2 line in error. The Southern Company's engine and two vehicles of the Great Western Company's train were damaged.

Datchet 13 May 1924

The engine of the 6.50am Staines to Windsor goods train was derailed after attempting to pass over points that had previously been damaged when they were run through. The Porter Signalman had replaced No 4 up line to up siding points prematurely during shunting operations whilst the locomotive was running round a draft of wagons standing in the up siding, having previously been placed there via No 9 points.

Fort Gomer Crossing between Fort Brockenhurst and Lee on Solent 20 May 1924

A collision occurred between the 6.15pm push & pull train from Fort Brockenhurst and a motor car driven by a Naval Lieutenant Commander which had stalled on the crossing. The car driver was seriously injured and removed to hospital by ambulance.

Irregularities in Working

Falmer 25th February 1924

The 8.45pm Eastbourne to Brighton passed Falmer up advance starting signal at danger without authority by one coach length. The signalman was also implicated by failing to apply signalling regulations 40a and 45a respecting the lowering of the home and starting signal as the train approached.

Purley Oaks 26 February 1924

The 8.23am Eastbourne to London Bridge passenger train passed Purley Oaks up main starting signal at danger without authority, being brought to a stand at South Croydon home signal.

Cannon Street 8 March 1924

The 3.30am Rotherhithe Road to Cannon Street empty train passed Cannon Street No 1 signal box No 7 line home signal at danger without authority by the engine and one coach length. The prompt action of the signalmen stopped the 4am Cannon Street to Dover leaving platform No 5 thus preventing a collision.

Cuxton Road 17 March 1924

At 1.47am the signalman at Cuxton Road irregularly replaced his signals in front of a light engine proceeding from Sole Street to Rochester because he failed to ascertain from the signalmen on either side the state of the block section before switching in the signal box. He also sent 'train out of section' for the light engine before it had passed his signal box.

New Cross 'A' and North Kent East 18 March 1924

A light engine which had been incorrectly coded by Orpington as for London instead of Bricklayers Arms was offered by New Cross 'A' signalman and accepted by North Kent East at 8.3pm The engine was then offered to Surrey Canal Junction and accepted on No 2 up line, and the North Kent East signal was lowered accordingly. Upon arrival at North Kent East home signal at 8.4pm the driver stopped and sounded the whistle code for Bricklayers Arms, whereupon the signalman at North Kent East replaced No 2 up line home signal. While this was happening New Cross 'A' signalman offered the 7.25pm Dartford to Charing Cross train and the signal lad at North Kent East, allegedly without the signalmen's knowledge, took it upon himself to remove the switch hook from the plunger and 'plunged' a free to New Cross 'A'. As soon as the signalmen at North Kent East realised what had occurred he sent 'Obstruction Danger' to New Cross A, but in haste the six beats were not given clearly and New Cross A did not acknowledge. However a telephone call made at the same time alerted the signalman at New Cross 'A' and the Dartford train was held at New Cross until the light engine had been properly disposed of. Initially the signalmen reported that one of them had stumbled and pressed the plunger accidentally but it emerged at the inquiry that they were making this statement to shield the signal lad.

Horley 20 March 1924

The signalman at Horley North irregularly sent 'train out of section' for the 4.10pm Norwood Junction to Three Bridges goods train which was standing on the down slow line between Horley North's home and starting signal (within the clearing point of the former). He then accepted the 6.8pm London Bridge to Brighton passenger train which came to a stand at the home signal 315 in the rear of the goods train.

Pluckley 24 March 1924

The 5.30 Dover Marine to Victoria passenger train passed the up home signal at danger without authority coming to a stand in the platform 468 yards ahead of the signal.

Norwood Junction 29 March 1924

The 12.15pm London Bridge to Victoria passenger train passed Norwood Junction South down local advanced starting signal at danger without authority, coming to a stand at Norwood Fork home signal. At the time of the irregularity the 11.58am London Bridge to Epsom Town passenger train was standing at Norwood Fork home signal awaiting acceptance, and fortuitously this was received in sufficient time to allow the train to proceed within the protection of the signal before the over-running train arrived at it. The inquiry questioned the guard of the 12:15pm train as to why he was not observing the signal and applying the brake when it became apparent that his train was disobeying it, but he stated that the tiny observatory lights fitted to 'Brighton' stock made this observation impossible. An investigation by the CME of the Brighton section stock observation lights is in hand.

Gloucester Road Junction 31 March 1934

The 12.18pm West Croydon to Crystal Palace train passed Gloucester Road Junction up West Croydon line home signal at danger without authority by 70 yards.

Queenborough 31 March 1924

The 12.50pm Queenborough to Swale Bridge materials train left Queenborough with the electric train staff applicable for the section Queenborough Station to Whiteway SB. The mistake was realised by the Queenborough signalman and arrangements made to transfer the correct staff to Swale and retrieve the wrong one It appears that there was a light engine waiting to proceed to Queenborough Pier at the same time and that both staffs were obtained, but handed to the wrong driver, who then failed to check that he had the correct one.

Polegate Crossing 13 April 1924

The driver of the 11:40pm New Cross Gate to Eastbourne Goods train was approaching Polegate Crossing with 49 wagons and a brake van, at 7.24am when he realised he was unable to stop at the down home signal which was at danger. He whistled to warn the signalman who promptly opened the crossing gates and who then sent 'train running away on right line' signal to Polegate West. At the time the 7.8am Eastbourne to Tunbridge Wells was standing in the station, so the Polegate West signalman reversed the points to direct the runaway towards the down loop line. He also offered the goods train to Polegate East who accepted it. It was found that the air glands on the engine and tender brake cylinders were leaking badly although the driver was aware of the reduction of brake efficiency before Lewes and should have taken action to rectify this sooner. The guard was also lacking in vigilance.

Beddington Lane 26 April 1924

The 11.10am Banstead to Beddington Lane ballast train entered the Engineer's Department sidings via No 5 Ground frame which were unlocked by the Beddington Lane to Waddon Marsh Electric Train Staff. On completion the ground frame was normalised and locked by the guard and the ganger then set off to return the train staff to Beddington Lane signal box. He was called back by another guard, this time in charge of the 8.30am Norwood Junction to Beddington Lane goods train, who requested the staff for shunting purposes. The 8.30am train guard then unlocked the ground frame with the staff and proceeded to shunt 35 wagons across to the opposite side of the single line into the Portland Cement sidings. He then uncoupled the engine and departed from the sidings, normalising the points and locking the ground frame, and with the intention of running light to Mitcham Junction for water he handed the staff to his driver. The driver immediately took the staff to Beddington Lane cabin and handed it to the signalman. As a consequence of the staff not being returned to the signalman after the 11.10am train had been put inside the Engineer's sidings, the signalman was unable to accept a passenger train from West Croydon and the 12.18pm Motor Train from West Croydon was delayed by 8 minutes. The electric train staff should also have been placed back in the instrument before being handed to the guard of the 8.30am train.

Fires on Company Premises

New Beckenham 1 March 1924

A stack of 60 creosoted sleepers lying near the line 200 yards south of New Beckenham caught fire and was eventually extinguished by the local fire brigade and by an off duty Traffic Inspector (who had first spotted the fire at 3.45pm from his house) and his neighbour who lived nearby. The cause was believed to be a spark from the engine of the 3.14pm Cannon Street to Addiscombe Road.

Kew Gardens 14 March 1924

At 7.30pm timber decking of the Thames River bridge was observed on fire. It was reported by the motorman of the 7.1pm ex Richmond Metropolitan District train at Gunnersbury. Local staff attended and extinguished it.

Barnham Junction 17 March 1924

When the 2.0pm Three Bridges to Fratton goods train was brought to a stand at Barnham Junction a fire was observed in GWR wagon No 87569 which was loaded with earthenware pipes packed with straw. Although the fire was quickly extinguished 87 pipes were damaged.

Crawley 20 March 1924

At 6.50am a fire occurred at Messrs Longley's Timber Works adjoining the line at Crawley. This rendered the line unsafe. Damage to Southern Railway Company property included sleepers charred, 200 rail keys charred and requiring replacement, 300 treenails likewise, 60 yards of boundary fence destroyed and several telegraph poles damaged and wires burnt; a down line stop signal was also damaged by fire.

Pouparts Junction 21starch 1924

At 12.42am fire was discovered and extinguished in planking on the four-span bridge north of the junction.

St Paul's 27 March 1924

At 11.50pm a fire was discovered in the Inspector's Office on the platform, and extinguished by the porter. Arson is assumed by no culprit so far identified.

Strawberry Hill 27 March 1924

At 6pm a fire was discovered in the station lamp room and quickly extinguished by staff. Three signal lamps, two gate lamps were badly burned and the inside of a cupboard charred.

West Norwood 3 April 1924

After the passage of the 9.24am Norwood Junction to Battersea Yard goods train the boards under the Booking Office and Waiting Room were found to be on fire. The outbreak was quickly extinguished. Traction current was cut off from 10.14am until 10.46am

Bournemouth Central 11 April 1924

At 9.0pm a wagon partially loaded with lime was observed to be on fire in Stonecrete Manufacturing Company's private siding, situated on the down side at the eastern end of the goods yard. The wagon was withdrawn and placed under the water column to extinguish the fire. The wagon sheet was destroyed and the wagon badly damaged. Spontaneous combustion of the load is suspected.

**South Eastern engine sheds:
Tonbridge 21 June 1958.**

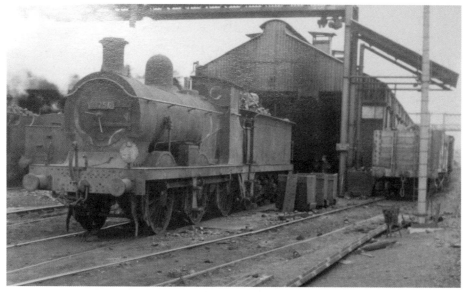

Faversham, 11 June 1959.

Ramsgate, 28 June 1959.

Between Haywards Heath and Wivelsfield 19 April 1924

A crate of paper inside a Pullman car of the 9.45am Victoria to Newhaven boat train was found on fire. It was quickly extinguished but two vestibule curtains were destroyed.

Woking 25 April 1924

A fire was observed in a first class compartment of a carriage standing in No 2 siding at 4.15am by a loco-man walking along the up yard. A mat in the compartment was well alight but staff attended and extinguished the fire. It is suspected that staff were using the vehicle improperly during the night, but no culprit has been identified.

Between Red Post Junction and Grateley 28 April 1924

At 7.45pm a permanent way hut on the up side was observed to be on fire, and was noticed by the crew of the 5.30pm Basingstoke to Salisbury goods train who stopped near staff cottages to report it. Before staff could attend, the fire had destroyed the hut. It is considered that sparks from a passing engine may have caught it alight.

Mishap in North Street Brighton 15 April 1924

A Southern Railway cart was delivering in Portland Street and whilst the carter was putting a chain on the wheel a large piece of paper was blown against the hind legs of the mare, causing her to bolt. The carter attempted to arrest her progress but before they reached the junction with North Street he was obliged to let go. The mare crossed North Street and collided with the shop window of Freeman Hardy & Willis boot shop. The animal was badly cut and the cart considerably damaged.

Burglary on Company Premises

Lewes 11 April 1924

The booking office was burgled during the night, by breaking a window. Only a bunch of keys were taken.

Larceny on Company Premises:

Barming Station 18 April 1924

On Good Friday evening at 4.35pm the Porter Signalman who was the sole member of staff on duty failed to lock the till and door in the booking office after booking passengers and left the station unlocked and unattended until 7pm On his return he found that cash parcels stamps and tickets had been stolen. Three lads have subsequently been apprehended by the police, and the tickets recovered.

Cost of Cartage

The Outdoor Manager had reported that a common figure for costs had been arrived at for all three sections. These are to take effect from 1 May 1924. The operating costs of Horse Cartage (both Goods and Parcels) will be worked out on the following basis:

HORSES

Average cost per week	London Goods and Parcels Horses			Country Goods and Parcels Horses		
	£	s	d	£	s	d
1 Interest and Depreciation	–	2	9	–	2	9
2 Fodder (including bedding saddlery etc.)	–	16	11½	–	16	11½
3 Shoeing	–	1	10	–	3	2
4 Superintendence	–		11	–		11
5 Stores (including water, lighting, heating, clothing, drugs and stationery)	–	1	4	–	1	4
6 Stabling		3	2½		3	7
7 Horsekeeping		10	9	*	1	4
TOTAL COST	1	17	9	1	10	½

*This amount represents proportion of Horsekeeper's wages incurred in London in connection with sick and spare horses only, in which must be added proportion of the wages of Stablemen where employed, based on the number of horses debited respectively to Goods and Parcels Cartage, also the wages of Stablemen and Carters in respect of Sunday stable duty.

ROAD VEHICLES (Horse Drawn)

Average cost per week 5s 0½ d

Annual cost of Clothing Supplied to Cartage Staff

London and Country Stations

	£	s	d
Inspector	6	18	7½
Foreman	6	19	0½
Carter	3	15	0
Van Lad	3	10	11½
Van Setter	3	10	11½

Revision of Passenger Services (Minute 4261)

A report was submitted by the Chief Operating Superintendent with particulars of various alterations in the train services operating from 1 and 4 May and 1 June respectively. Details of the alterations are appended to the minutes, the effect on the train mileages being as follows:

Miles per week

	Steam	Electric	Total
Weekdays			
Increase to operate from 1 May	917	–	917
Sundays			
Increase to operate from 4 May	1,420	1,605	3,025
Increase to operate from 1 June	977	–	977
Totals	**3,314**	**1,605**	**4,919**

These figures are embodied in the summary relating to the Summer train alterations dealt with below.

Reports were also submitted from the Chief Operating Superintendent on the subject of the revisions in the Passenger Train services to operate on and from Monday 14 July.

The general effect thereof is shewn in the following table:

Miles per Week (including Sundays)

	Electric	Steam	Total
Summer Services – 1923	92,990	*651,676	*744,666
Summer Services Special Mileage †	–	7,842	7,842
Summer Services Gross Total	92,990	659,518	752,508
Present service (including alterations made since October 1923)	93,020	622,307	715,327
Proposed Summer Service 1924	92,663	664,566	757,229
Increase to operate on 14 July	–	42,259	41,902
Decrease to operate on 14 July	357	–	
Increase compared with Summer 1923	–	5,048	4,721
Decrease compared with Summer 1923	327	–	

*Includes (for comparison purposes) miles on lines taken over during year, ie 12,000 miles for the Isle of Wight, Lynton and Barnstaple, and Callington Lines.

†Comprises mileage of special trains run regularly during Summer 1923, the equivalent of which has been embodied in the proposals for the Ordinary Summer Service 1924

Additional Staff for Summer Traffic

A report was submitted from the Chief Operating Superintendent shewing the additional staff required in his department in connection with the summer traffic as per the following list:

	1924	Net increase over 1923
Clerks	120	8
Inspectors	2	–
Station Foremen	5	2
Foremen Ticket Collector	1	–
Ticket Collectors	40	–
Toll Collector	1	–
Excess Luggage Collectors	10	–
Parcels Porters	28	7
Junior Parcels Porters	3	–
Porters Grade 2	200	9
Junior Porters	5	–
Porter, Grade 1	1	–
Goods Porters	25	–
Cloak Room Attendants	13	–
Ladies Waiting Room Attendants	13	–
Messengers	2	–
Shunters	13	1
Signalmen	6	–
Porter Signalmen	2	–
Porter Guards	27	–
Carriage Cleaners	27	3
Crane Driver	1	–
Working Foreman	1	–
Carters	29	–
Halt Keeper	1	–
Horse Keepers	4	–
H. P. Vanmen	3	–
Checkers	5	–
Time Keeper	1	–
Lampman	1	–
Trace Horse Boy	1	–
Crossing Keeper	1	–
	567	**31**

Waterloo & City Railway

A report from the Chief Operating Superintendent has been submitted with a revised proof Book of Instructions applicable to the Waterloo & City line. It is recommended that the Book as revised is authorised for issue to the staff.

Ilfracombe Town Office

Referring to Minute No 3965 of 1 October 1923 under which a Joint Enquiry Office was instituted at Ilfracombe during last summer, it was reported that arrangements have been made in conjunction with the Great Western Company, for a similar

Above: **Bexhill West, 16 May 1964.**

The erstwhile Lynton & Barnstaple Railway. (Ensure you are aware of the stunning new work by Tony Nicholson on this line and now available!)

Joint Office during the ensuing summer at some premises in the Market Square, which have been offered to the Companies by the Council at a rental of £20 for four months commencing 1 June. It is recommended that the arrangement be adopted and that the expenses of the Office be borne by the two Companies in ratio to the number of tickets issued from such Office by the respective Companies' routes via Barnstaple.

Telephone Facilities at Lynton

Representations have been received from the Lynton Urban District Council in regard to the provision of a Post Office telephone at the Station. Such facility existed prior to the War, and it is recommended that the telephone be reinstated at a rental payable to the Post Office of £7 per annum.

Billingshurst Mr A. C. Puttock's Application

Under an agreement dated 20 October 1915 a siding was provided for Mr. A. C. Puttock at Billingshurst. This gentleman has now converted his business into a Limited Liability Company known as Puttock & Wesson Ltd and it is recommended that the benefits of the agreement in question are transferred to this firm.

Polegate Brick and Tile Company's siding, Polegate

The above firm desire that facilities shall be given for the Southdown Tileries Company's traffic at this siding, and it is recommended that this be acceded to upon the same terms and conditions as apply to the traffic of the Polegate firm, vide Agreement with the Company dated 15 February 1921.

Messrs Whitehead & Company's siding, Portland

A report has been submitted by the Chief Commercial Manager to the effect that the above mentioned firm went into liquidation in March 1921 and the works have now been disposed of to a new Company, viz, the Whitehead Torpedo Company Ltd. It is recommended that the benefits of an agreement between the Great Western and South Western Railways and Messrs Whitehead & Company dated 9 May 1906, 28 September 1915 and 22 November 1917 also Memorandum dated 21 February 1916 be transferred to the Whitehead Torpedo Company.

Surplus Appliances

Whitstable Harbour Crossover Road and No 17 Shunt Signal

The connection between the platform line and the 'back road' at Whitstable Harbour together with No 17 shunt signal is not required and it is recommended that they be removed. Estimated original cost £156, estimated cost of removal and making good £107, estimated value of recovered materials £9, estimated annual savings of maintenance £6, Estimated annual savings of renewals based on assumed life £8.

Porton Siding

The short siding on the down side of the line at the eastern end of the station is no longer required, and it is recommended that it be removed. Estimated original cost £178, estimated cost of removal and making good £102, estimated value of recovered materials £33, estimated annual savings of maintenance £16, estimated annual savings of renewals based on assumed life £30.

New Works

The following new works are recommended.

Blackfriars

Renewal of front wall and roof and various other improvements in the Delivery Office. Provision of four additional lamps on the 'back road'.

Estimated cost £914

Northam Sidings

Provision of an electric gantry. A saving of £770 per annum is ultimately estimated.

Estimated cost £1,735, to be charged to New Works Revenue Suspense Account and written off in three years.

Another Special Train in Colour

On Saturday 23 March 1963 the Railway Enthusiasts Club organised and ran another special using pull-push fitted 'M7' No 30108 and coach Set No 608 (vehicles 6689 and 1330) together with pull/push open third No 1343*. It was an ambitious operation starting from Farnborough and initially to Basingstoke and down the stub of the former Basingstoke & Alton railway as far as Thorneycroft's siding. Returning to Basingstoke the train set out for Grateley before turning north to Amesbury and Bulford. Back at Grateley it was west now to Salisbury and a shunt move into the former GWR terminus which had ceased to be used as a passenger station in 1932. From Salisbury it was on now to Southampton Central via Romsey and Redbridge. At Southampton Central the plan had been to travel via Shawford Junction and the Didcot,

Newbury & Southampton (DNS) line to Reading Central (Coley) goods, but this was altered at short notice due to the derailment of a tanker train on the DNS between Highclere and Burghclere. Instead the special went straight up the main line to Reading via Basingstoke. Yet still there was more to come, as leaving Coley goods the train continued – locomotive leading – through Reading General and thence via the connection to the SR lines at Reading Old Junction and on to the Southern destined for Wokingham and Ascot. Here the train took the Guildford line platform before completing its trip via Frimley and Sturt Lane West Junction back on to the South Western main line and the final few miles back east to Farnborough where the tour terminated. In total something in the order of 170-plus miles in a little over nine hours

*No 1343 had come from Set 607 which had been damaged in an accident at Eastbourne sidings in September 1961, the corresponding brake composite being withdrawn. (With grateful thanks to Mike King for coach information.)

At the start of the tour around 9.15am. No 30108 carries a Bournemouth, '71B', shedcode which was from where most of the pull-push fitted members of the class working the former South Western lines were then based. A goodly supply of coal will be noted – it would be needed! *Trevor Owen/Hugh Davies*

Above: **Another view prior to leaving. 'M7' No 30108 is waiting in the former military platforms at Farnborough ready to depart west.** *Trevor Owen/Hugh Davies*

Finally it seemed the train was ready, plenty of steam and the all-important headboard – how often in life did an 'M7' carry such an embellishment? Notice in the background the lower quadrant LSWR signals, part of the pneumatic installation between Brookwood and Basingstoke. After a bright start the weather has also started to change ... *Roger Holmes*

The excellent 'Six Bells Junction' website gives the schedule for the service but on this occasion not the actual times. What we do know is that Basingstoke was due to be reached in 23 minutes from Farnborough and where the train would wait for five minutes. It would then set off in the direction of Alton travelling as far as the remaining track permitted, vis-à-vis, the Thorneycroft siding. Here was a scheduled wait and photographic stop of seven minutes. In this first view, the train is seen cautiously descending the steep gradient and sharp curve which takes the erstwhile light railway away from the main line and past the Waterworks pumping station. As can be seen a headboard was provided at both ends of the train. Under normal circumstances the Thorneycroft siding was shunted on an 'as required' basis from Basingstoke. Today, more than half a century later, there is still a short length of disused track at the west end of the down yard that can be seen curving away towards Alton although it is many years since any rail vehicle ventured that way. Folklore has it that when it was still connected to the rest of the yard a curious driver of a Class 47 ventured down the bank slightly before changing his mind and returning to the yard, likely the one and only time any form of diesel traction ever traversed even part of the former Basingstoke & Alton (B&A) line. *Trevor Owen/Hugh Davies*

Below and opposite: **Two views now of the train at the siding. The first shows the service under Worting Road bridge, literally the end of the line, and then slightly forwards. No steps were provided to alight and rejoin the trains, instead a 'degree of agility' was required some years before Health and Safety would have totally prohibited such activities so far as the public were concerned.** *both Trevor Owen/Hugh Davies*

Leaving the B&A, the train returned to Basingstoke and was due to set off for Grateley at 10.15. Forty-two minutes later, including a four-minute stop at Andover (water perhaps?), it arrived at Grateley where it turned on to the Amesbury–Bulford line – officially closed to all traffic a few weeks earlier on 4 March 1963. Here the special is seen approaching Amesbury on what had originally been double track but was singled in October 1953 – a full history of the Amesbury to Bulford line together with its various sidings and connections is available – *Rails Across the Plain: The Amesbury & Bulford Railway*, by Jeffery Grayer, published by Noodle Books ISBN 978190641956. *Trevor Owen/Hugh Davies*

We now see Amesbury with the special train having just left for Bulford. Note Amesbury's 'unique' scaffold-type canopy and open footbridge. The site was very much in its last days at this time: a far cry from the time when thousands of troops would use the facility.

The service has now arrived at Bulford, the limit of the tour, although beyond which the railway had once continued on to Ratfyn, Sling, Rollestone, Larkhill and the Fays branch. These extensions were only ever worked by the military and had been closed in stages some time before passenger working ceased to Bulford. Here at Bulford, facilities had always been spartan: an exposed windswept platform, wide enough for a considerable number of soldiers, and basically that was it. Originally worked by tablet between Amesbury and Bulford, this was replaced by 'No signalman key token' from as early as April 1935. Likely both crew and passengers were glad to rejoin the train at departure time. *both Roger Holmes*

The train is now back at Amesbury, evidence of previous traffic visible from what were the three platform faces provided here. Notice also the turntable which required the use of extension bars when engines the size of a Mogul needed turning. *Roger Holmes*

We are now back at Grateley on the main west of England line and it appears almost ready for departure again – judging by the running photographer. Years earlier Grateley had been the location chosen for the first experiments with the low-pressure automatic signalling installed by the LSWR. The station remains open today but is unstaffed and reduced to 'basic' status. *Roger Holmes*

In the photographers involved we end with the best of both worlds: Roger Holmes was travelling and Trevor Owen chasing the special by road. Here we have two of Trevor's images showing the train passing Tunnel Junction just east of Salisbury and then disappearing into Salisbury Tunnel. The junction with the line from Romsey is also clearly seen. *Trevor Owen/Hugh Davies*

Above: **We have no images of the train at Salisbury and instead we next pick it up steaming well as it passes through Dunbridge en-route to Southampton.** *Trevor Owen/Hugh Davies*

An unscheduled stop at Platform 2 at Southampton Central. The booked time for here shows the service as 'passing at 2.38 pm', almost exactly what the clock shows on the tower, although clearly a stop was being made. *Roger Holmes*

With the light now becoming less ideal for photography the train is seen on the up main at Shawford Junction and with the signals off for a run via Winchester City instead of the planned DNS line. The home signal for up trains on to the DNS route is the one showing 'on' on the bracket. The line on the left is the down goods loop for trains coming off the DNS. *Trevor Owen/Hugh Davies*

Another water stop, this time in the up platform line at Micheldever, for many years a holding location for rolling stock either withdrawn or pending works. This is typified in the background by what appears to be a former SECR 10-compartment vehicle displaying the dreaded condemned symbol. Shortly afterwards, upon arrival at Basingstoke, the train was shunted into the former GWR station for another photo stop. *Roger Holmes*

We next catch up with our train passing Mortimer (between Basingstoke and Southcote Junction–Reading) and seemingly travelling at a reasonable rate. This section of line had been GWR and then BR(W) until 1950, evidence of this seen in the paint colours of the signal box– that is with the exception of the box name which is a standard white on green enamel sign. Shortly after this came the visit to Coley Goods before returning to the Berks & Hants to reach Reading General and pass under the GW main lines to reach Southern metals once again. *both Trevor Owen/Hugh Davies*

With the light fading the opportunity for further photography was probably limited, although Trevor did record the two rose embellishments that were added at some stage to the cabside number of No 30108. (Whether this was just on the one side is not known.) No 30108 would carry these pieces as a momento of the day until it was withdrawn in May 1964 and scrapped in the autumn of the same year. *Trevor Owen/Hugh Davies*

Tragedy at Bramshott Halt, 5 August 1939
As reported in the
Farnborough Chronicle & Fleet Times
Submitted by Martin Burrell

Bramshott Halt on 8 May 1954 with an REC special. (For full stock details see Mike King's excellent *Southern Vans and Coaches in Colour*.)

Terrible Railway Fatality: Workmen mowed down by express at Fleet/Reckless crowd rush across lines.

After listening to evidence for more than two hours and consulting in private for seven minutes, a coroner's jury at Fleet on Wednesday found that the three London men who lost their lives in the tragic accident on the main railway line at Bramshott Halt on Saturday were accidentally killed.

The three men were John Graham Mallon (30), an electrician of 34 Chadworth Buildings, Lever Street, EC, Isaac Michael Musaphia (23), motor driver, of 21 Brunswick Buildings, Goulston Street, Whitechapel, and Frederick Donovan (22), bricklayer of 92 Westminster Bridge Road.

The three men were employed on the building of the new Army barracks at Southwood Farm, Cove, where about 3.000 men are employed and were among a large number of men who were on the platform at and near the Bramshott Halt on Saturday afternoon awaiting the special train to take them back to London. It appears that the up platform was packed with men and there were men on the down platform, and others were walking along the lines from the direction of the camp towards the Halt. At this point the railway runs in a straight line for well over a mile. A fourth man, Thomas Harris, of 3 Artillery Passage, London E1, was taken to Fleet Hospital with internal injuries. It was stated yesterday (Thursday) that he is progressing favourably.

A Dangerous Habit

According to evidence given at the inquest, some hundreds of men working on the camp have been coming from London and elsewhere by special trains daily and been in the habit of crossing the line to reach the platforms rather than take the longer journey under the bridge and along the Cove–Fleet road.

Caught by Express

That apparently is what happened on Saturday. As the empty workmen's train came to the up platform to take men to London, a crowd started to board it, others rushed across the line from the down side. At that moment the Jersey boat express which runs non-stop from Southampton Docks to Waterloo, came along at a speed of more than 60mph. Most of the men saw the express in time, but the train caught the three deceased men and literally cut them to pieces.

The Inquest

The inquest was held at the Fleet Council Offices on Wednesday by Mr H. M. Foster, the district coroner, and a jury of whom Mr F. S. Mann was foreman.

Mr Harry Rose appeared for the relatives of Mr Musaphia, Mr Kirk Glazebrook for the contractors, Sir Lindsay Parkinson & Co Ltd, Mr J. Benstead for the NUR, and Mr J. H. Jones for the Southern Railway Co.

Coroner's Opening Address

Addressing the jury, the Coroner said the three men were employed on the new barracks and, with many others, were returning to London after having finished their work by special train about 4.30pm. '1 won't go into great detail now', said the Coroner. 'I will say what may appear necessary later on, after you have heard the evidence, if further remarks are necessary. These men crossed the two down lines and the through up line. Apparently a down express went by them,' said the Coroner after describing the layout of the railway track, 'and they passed behind that to go to the train which was on the up local line, the one nearest to the road, and they were knocked down and killed by an express train which was going towards London on the through line, that is, next to the line on which the train they were trying to get into was standing.

Evidence of Identification

Frank Mallon, of Lever Street, Clerkenwell, a brother of John Mallon, who gave evidence of identification, said he was able to do so without any doubt. His brother was a fit and healthy man in every respect.

The witness said he was on the station platform at the time, and in reply to Mr Rose said there were over a hundred men crossing the line at the time.

Joseph Musaphia of 36 Solebay Street, Mile End, who identified his brother's remains from the clothing and other things, said he was a motor driver and a fit and healthy man.

Joseph Ryan, of 92 Westminster Bridge Road who identified Donovan, said he was able to do so by his clothing and a scar on his back. He was a bricklayer and a fit and healthy man.

Medical Evidence

Dr Harold Greenish stated that he had reached the scene of the accident at ten minutes to five on Saturday afternoon. He saw one body between the two centre lines, by the platform, another on the grass nearer the London end and a third by a cottage. He thought they had been moved, but was not sure. All were dead.

The bodies were very severely mutilated consistent with having been knocked down by a train.

Mr Rose: 'Could you say which body was in each place?' – 'I could not. There were so many pieces that I did not ask anything about each individual. I examined them more carefully afterwards in the mortuary.'

At this stage Mr Jones put in plans of Bramshott Halt area which were handed to the members of the jury for their guidance.

Stationmaster's Evidence

Sydney Dunn, stationmaster at Farnborough, stated that he reached Bramshottt Halt about 4.30 on Saturday afternoon. He found the up platform crowded with men to its fullest extent. There were men sitting on the edge of the platform on the down side, and men who had been sitting on the edge of the platform on the up side who moved away as the train in which he was riding approached them. He also saw about 200 men walking in the recess alongside the down local line, going towards the Halt from the direction of the camp.

'What time was the train due to start for Waterloo?' – 'I came up with the empty stock from Fleet which was due to start about 4.30.'

Warned to 'Stand Back'

'When it came to a standstill, what happened?' – 'I saw the men crossing the line, and I waved my arms from the engine cab and said "Stand back," but they took no notice of that.

'As soon as the train stopped all the doors were opened and there was a struggle to get in on the platform side. Some ran down off the platform in front of the train to get in on the down side.'

'You say you shouted. Do you think they heard you?' – 'I don't think so. They were making a lot of noise.'

'What other railway servants were on the platform?' – 'There was a porter at the front end and a man at the back of the train with a red flag to make sure no one got behind the train and to stop anything from coming along if he could.'

Climbing in on the Wrong Side

'Did you yourself see some of the men climbing in the train on the wrong side?' – 'Yes.'

'What happened next?' – 'I got off the engine on the platform side and before I could get round to the front to see what the men were doing, and do what I could to keep them away, the express came through. I heard one or two thuds and knew what had happened.'

Stopped the Traffic

'I went to see what had happened and to help up the injured men. Looking up the line I could see other bodies. Meanwhile the express had gone on towards Farnborough. Word had been given and the next trains were stopped. I could see a train was stopped at Fleet and I went to the telephone to get doctors and ambulances and advise all concerned. The nearest telephone was at the golf house at Bramshott.'

Had Expected an Accident

The Coroner: 'Had you been there on many previous occasions when the men go in these special trains?' – 'Yes. The station master at Fleet and I take it alternately.'

'Had the same rush across the line taken place?' – 'It always takes place. Last Saturday there was a rush of traffic, being the Saturday before the Bank Holiday.'

'Had it given you a certain amount of anxiety that there might be accidents of this kind?' – 'I have expected one a good many times before.'

Would Not Keep off the Line

'Had you done all you could to remedy the conditions with the staff at your disposal?' – 'Yes. We have had the police there to warn the men to move back, but as soon as he moved from one place to another they would move back again. They kept see-sawing and would not keep off the line.'

'Had you reported the matter to the higher authorities of the railway?' – 'Yes. A report was sent every time I went there, to the London West Divisional Superintendent.'

'Did you have any reply from him?' – 'Necessary steps had been taken. They sent police down occasionally.'

No Need to go on Line

Mr Jones: 'Which is the way the men should take to the Halt?' – 'They can leave the camp, go under the bridge, and walk up the road.'

'There was no necessity for them to be on the line?' – 'No.'

Notice Posted

'Are there very big notices all along the line?' – 'Yes.'

'Is there one in particular by the bridge?' – 'There is one big one which says the way to the station is under the bridge and along the road.'

The witness said the up platform will take eight coaches easily and would accommodate 1,500 people. Six special trains were run for these men on Saturday.

'How many people can go on a train?' – 'They pack into the first one if they can.'

'Is that what they were trying to do on this occasion?' – 'Yes, and they were jammed in as hard as they could.'

'Have you any idea what advantage there could be in rushing across from the down side to the off-side of the train?' – 'Only that they were trying to get one back on those who were getting in the other way.'

Repeated Warnings

'Have you yourself warned these men?' 'Until I cannot speak.'

In reply to Mr Rose, the witness said that this Saturday was the first day on which the Jersey express had come along at that particular time.

'Did you think it necessary to tell the men they were not to dangle their legs over the platform?' – 'I was not there to tell them, but, I am sure the porter had done so previously, according to the usual experience.'

During Mr Rose's cross-examination of the witness, the Coroner interrupted and said the jury were only enquiring into the cause of death.

Mr Rose: 'I am trying to point out it was not necessarily the crossing of the line that brought about these deaths.'

The Coroner allowed the cross-examination to continue.

Nearly Crushed to Death

'They were crowded in?' asked Mr Rose. 'They positively swarmed in, did they?'

'Yes' replied Mr Dunn. 'I got in once and nearly got crushed to death. They run across, open the doors on the offside, and get in.'

The Porter's Warning

Albert Edward Lipscombe, porter at Fleet Station, said he went on duty at Bramshott Halt at 4.15pm, on Saturday and put out his bicycle on the down platform. He looked to the up platform and saw 800 to 1,000 men there. There were about 100 men on the down platform, and others were walking along the down line, going from the direction of the camp towards the platform. He saw men sitting on both platforms with their legs dangling over the edges. He walked along the up line and told them to stand back as there were many trains about that particular time. Some moved back and some did not. When he got to the London end he looked round, and there were then about 150 men on the down side. He saw the empty train leave Fleet station, and saw that a train was signalled up and another down. He got on to the through road and shouted as hard as he could to tell everyone to keep back as there would probably be three trains at the Halt about the same time. The down train came first, and he continued to shout to the men until it came through.

Just after the down express passed the workmen's train came into the platform. He then saw men on the down local track and some on the up through. He continued to tell the men to keep back. As the workmen's train was stopping at the platform the boat train came through. When it reached the bridge he gave a last shout to the men to keep back and jumped out of the way. He was then on the edge of the local line.

'At that time were men running across the tracks?' – 'Yes.'

The witness said that up to a week before Saturday there were fewer men and fewer trains, and conditions were not so bad.

No Means of Keeping the Men Out

A juryman suggested that when the platform was full, steps might be taken to keep others from reaching it. The witness replied that there was plenty of room on the banks.

The Coroner: 'Was there any means without having a regiment of soldiers there, of keeping these men out of the station?' – 'No. They climbed through the wire on both sides and broke the fences.' 'They came from everywhere in large numbers?' – 'Yes.'

Express Driver's Evidence

Edward John Diment, the driver of the Jersey boat train, said he passed through Fleet station on the up through line, at 60 to 65 miles per hour. Approaching the bridge at Bramshott Halt he saw a number of men crossing the rails. He opened the whistle before he reached the bridge and it remained open until he was nearly half way to the stationary train. There were about 40 or 50 men on the line then.

'Did you notice anything unusual about the offside of the stationary train?' – 'Yes. I saw about seven doors open and men scrambling into the train.' 'What did you do after whistling?' – 'I applied my brake. I knew I should knock some of the men down I could not help myself.' The witness said the weather and visibility were good. The boat runs at different times and is not a daily train.

Swarming Across the Lines

Hugh Edward Sutton of Earley stated that on Saturday afternoon he was motoring and stopped at Bramshott Bridge. He saw an empty train come in on the up line. The up platform was crowded, and there were 100 to 150 men on the down platform. As the empty train was stopping he saw 30 or 40 men jump from the down platform, cross the three sets of lines and those in front started to scramble into the train. As they were crossing the line an express came through and the men scattered. Most of them went back, but a few went on to the up line and started to get into the workmen's train. After the down express had passed the men who had gone back crossed the up line and joined the others who were getting into the train. As they were doing so, the up express came through. That

was about half a minute after the down express had passed.

The witness said there were a lot of men walking on the line from the direction of Farnborough in addition to others crossing the line.

William Loney, a carpenter, living in London, who was in the garden of Railway Cottage adjacent to the up platform, gave evidence that the up platform was crowded with workmen and that the down platform was about a quarter full, and that men crossed the lines to get into the train.

The Coroner's Summing Up

Addressing the jury at the conclusion of the evidence, the Coroner said he thought that, considering there must have been a certain amount of confusion at the spot, it was extraordinary how consistent the evidence had been with very few discrepancies. He thought what happened was abundantly clear from the evidence. He pointed out that a Coroner's inquest is held simply to ascertain the cause of death, of which there was no doubt in this case. Beyond that their only duty was to ascertain whether there was any criminal negligence on the part of anyone except the deceased men themselves. After defining criminal negligence, the Coroner said that the Railway Company, or at any rate, the staff on the spot, appeared to have done all they could to warn the men.

Trespass at Own Risk

After all they are not children, he said, they know what a railway is and that they will get hurt should a train hit them. Those who trespass on the railway do so at their own risk. The coroner added that warnings had been given repeatedly and were disregarded. He hoped that this unfortunate case would be a warning to others.

Jury Apportions No Blame

The jury, after an absence of seven minutes, returned a verdict of accidental death and the Foreman commentated that they apportioned no blame. Mr Jones, on behalf of the Railway Company, expressed their sympathy with the relatives of the deceased and similar expressions were made by Mr Glazebrook and Mr Benstead. The Coroner concurred on behalf of himself and the jury, and thanked the Railway company for their assistance to him. (The location does appear in *Jowett's Railway Atlas* but was certainly extant, albeit unused, until at least 1964. Do not confuse this Bramshott with the location of the same name near Hindhead. Some images of the location the subject of this article may also be found at http://www.historicfarnborough.co.uk/Bramshothalt.html.)

Terry Cole's Rolling Stock Files
No 38 and 39

[All photos Terry Cole Collection]

Part 1: Three LSWR Vehicles

A reasonable number of pre-Grouping vehicles could still be seen on British Railways in the 1950s although their numbers were rapidly declining and many had been relegated to Departmental use.

Above: **Here is ex London & South Western Railway 10-ton 5-plank open wagon SR No 3872 still in Southern Railway livery recorded at Nine Elms in April 1957. It is one of 25 built around 1910 to SR Diagram 1313 and is an example of the final development of the LSWR 10-ton open.**

Right: **Twenty-six 10-ton ballast brake vans were built by the LSWR around 1909 and given Diagram 1736 by the Southern. This is No 61925, branded 'New Cross Gate Outdoor Machinery Department' seen here at Brighton in March 1956.**

Many of the LSWR 10-ton box vans ended up in Departmental Service, a typical example being No DS1718 as seen here at Brighton in February 1951. It is branded 'To work between Eastleigh Loco Shed and Brighton Running Shed', its purpose being the transfer of spares, stores and other material.

Part 2: 2 LBSCR Goods Vehicles and an 'odd man out'

On the mainland ex London, Brighton & South Coast Railway vehicles were not particularly numerous in British Railways days, many having been transferred to the Isle of Wight. The box vans in particular often ended up as grounded bodies in use as stores in goods yards.

Permanent Way vehicles often had longer lives. Here is an ex LBSCR 3-plank 15-ton drop-side ballast wagon, No S62764, at Brighton in May 1953. Built around 1906/8, these vehicles were given SR Diagram No1754. The vehicle is branded 'Three Bridges Material Depot'.

This is 8-ton box van No 46680 at Nine Elms in April 1957 and it appears still to be in traffic use. It is one of 98 such vans built by contractors in 1920 with a steel underframe. The Southern allocated them Diagram 1434.

And now for something completely different. This deliciously antiquated specimen, No E6304E, is in the middle of a van train at Victoria in June 1957. It is an ex Midland & Great Northern Railway six-wheeled passenger brake van complete with side duckets. So, modellers, if the 50s is your period, literally anything goes!

The Lost Archives of Stephen Townroe
Part 5

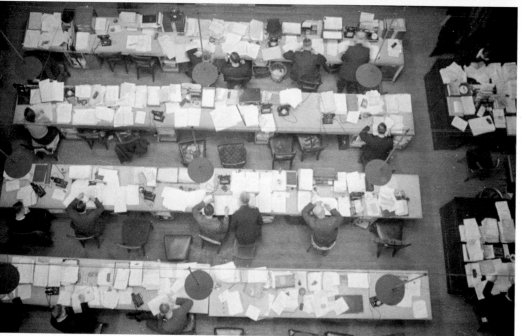

Above: **Commencing this issue's trawl through the archive we have a view of what is referred to as the 'Woking Divisional HQ Loco'. We know this image was taken some time between January and June 1940 and in a building that displays little if any apparent ARP protection. Might this even have been the office for the Woking area, perhaps located at Deepdene? No names of persons seen are given – but oh to be able to read some of paperwork scattered around … !**

Left: **This view is of the 'Pool Room' at Deepdene. No doubt taken from one of galleries, it also gives a small sense of the opulence that had once existed at this palatial mansion. We are not told which office this represented.**

A study in concentration, captioned as 'Deepdene, temporary offices in use for the first winter of the war'. Although we are not told which department was involved, there must be every likelihood this was related to SCT's 'familiar turf', vis-à-vis Motive Power.

On 27 March 1940 the right-hand smoke deflector from No 787 (see also illustration on page 14), came loose between Tisbury and Dinton, striking another train passing in the opposite direction. We are not given details of the other train or damage that must have occurred. No 787 was taken off its train at the first opportunity and was then recorded with a number of missing bolts also highlighted. With these essential parts missing it is likely the plate was reasonably fine until turbulence was created by the passing of the other train, causing it to flap. There would of course have been an enquiry, likely focusing on the condition and examination of the locomotive at the start of its journey. The results are not reported.

Above: Likely taken when SCT was perhaps on his way to Deepdene via the South Western main line. Taken from a slower moving train, he is about to be overtaken by a 'Lord Nelson' working a West of England service. Notice also the smoke deflectors are doing their job as intended and that the engine is fitted with the Bulleid large diameter chimney associated with the fitment of a Lemaître exhaust with multiple jet blastpipes.

A view of the new locomotive running offices at Deepdene as provided sometime prior to June 1940. Perhaps not in exact keeping with the architectural style of the original 18th century mansion, it was practicalities that were more important in 1940 – clearly the lion guarding the building was not amused either!

We now have a series of images of moving trains taken at Woking at the point where the LSWR main line and Portsmouth direct diverge. All were recorded in the months leading up to July 1940 which makes these all the more unusual. SCT clearly had access to film – we know he took record views on his various official travels around the system at this time, so it is likely he was provided with this essential for the purpose – but also took the opportunity to record a few general views at the same time! No specific locomotive or train workings are given.

We now have a small series of three images showing the junction of the Portsmouth Direct with the main line just east of Havant. The first is looking east and shows the Warblington up (left) and down (right) sidings parallel with the main line. The view is east towards Warblington with the physical junction just behind the camera. Next is the junction and what may well be the reason for the images, namely the new footbridge over the Portsmouth Direct. This time the siding on the left is the headshunt for Havant goods yard. Finally looking west, we see Havant station and the busy level crossing at the east end of the station. Again no specific date, although we know the series was taken sometime before July 1940.

Two more staff views now. The first is of a '… labourer on volunteer Home Guard duties', we are not told where. Perhaps slightly more interesting is another view of Deepdene, this time showing the 'Locomotive Controllers' at work in the main hall; again no names are given. Note the 'Railway Service' lapel badge worn by the man on the telephone.

But it was not all office work, for SCT was sent to Betchworth near Dorking in October 1940 to supervise the re-railing of a 'Q' class 0-6-0 which had fallen into a bomb crater, The two cranes seen were respectively of 36- and 45-ton capacity. It is possible to identify the 45T crane as No 1561S delivered to the SR from Ransomes & Rapier on 23 July 1940 and at the time based at Guildford. Studied closely, several members of the 'bowler hat' brigade may be seen.

The senior staff, of which SCT was one, was evidently reasonably well looked after at Deepdene and no doubt also appreciated this – as witness this view of 'Fred the waiter'. There was also time for some light-hearted moments with this photograph which was captioned: 'The Loco show, my cardboard engine'. Taken sometime prior to July 1941, 'SCT' is the driver complete with his trademark pipe. Might this even have been an intended SCT design … ?

To be continued in the next issue.

Spithead 1937

Richard Halton

SOUTHERN RAILWAY STEAMERS WITH ADMIRALTY GUESTS AT NAVAL REVIEW - SPITHEAD, 1935

THE NAVAL REVIEW MAY 20TH 1937
SEE THE BRITISH FLEET
& WARSHIPS OF OTHER NATIONS
SPECIAL TRAINS AND FARES by SOUTHERN RAILWAY
Ask for Naval Review programme obtainable from S·R Enquiry Offices or Agencies

At 7.05 am on the morning of Thursday 20 May 1937 a special excursion train left Platform 14 of London's Victoria station bound for the south coast. The train had a capacity of 540 passengers, who disembarked at Portsmouth and Southsea station just over two hours later to transfer to a paddle steamer to view the ships assembled for the Coronation Naval Review at Spithead. Their ship was PS *Medway Queen* and 80 years ago the crowd of people on board were marvelling at the array of naval might assembled between Portsmouth and the Isle of Wight. Besides the Royal Navy there were ships representing many other countries,

some of whom would become allies in a few short years' time and others who would be opponents. The party returned in the early hours of the following day, leaving Portsmouth and Southsea at 2.27am and arriving back at Victoria at 4.25am. The event being celebrated was, of course, the Coronation of King George VI which had taken place on the 12 May at Westminster Abbey.

The special traffic notices for the day(s) contain a wealth of detail regarding not only the chartered trains that ran from London but also the excursion ships, plying their trade amongst the fleet in connection with that railway traffic. Most train departures were from Waterloo but a few, including the *Medway Queen's* train, ran from Victoria. In 1937 many of

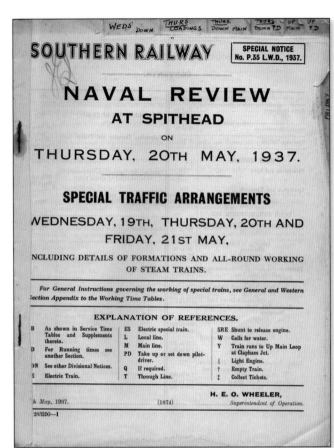

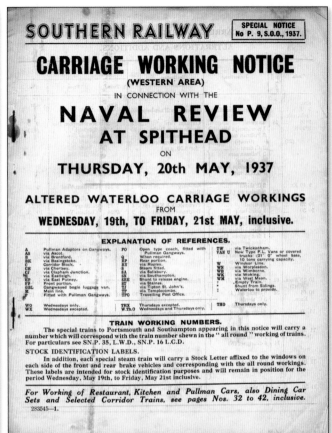

these excursion ships and ferries were paddle steamers with only a few being motor driven screw ships. Some were allocated places in the fleet to be reviewed, others were simply there as excursion vessels. It is likely that passengers on the latter had a better view of the proceedings although all would have steamed through the assembled fleet at some stage.

As to the fleet itself, the official programme contains a detailed list of the naval and merchant vessels in the Review fleet and a plan of the anchorage. The Royal Navy component included no less than 10 battleships and battle cruisers including HMS *Hood*, five aircraft carriers and 16 cruisers besides countless destroyers, submarines and other craft. The *Admiral Graf Spee* from Germany was probably the best known foreign warship and there were others, of course, from the USA (*New York*), France (*Dunkerque*), Russia (*Marat*), Japan (*Asigara*) and a host of other navies.

A few trains were run on the day before the review, Wednesday 19 May. Some of these connected with the large ships involved, others with SR or Isle of Wight Steam Packet Co vessels. One was from Woking at 10.15am to Portsmouth Harbour and connected with PS *Sandown*. It was booked for 'SR' and so is likely that this was a day trip to see the ships before the main event and was, perhaps, for the benefit of staff or the nearby Southern Railway Childrens' Home. The big operation commenced early on the Thursday morning and the Special Traffic Arrangements detail no less than 65 special train workings, mainly from Waterloo and Victoria. The trains ran

to Portsmouth Harbour, Portsmouth and Southsea or Southampton Docks, either right into the docks or to the Millbrook (western dock) Entrance. Only a couple were routed to Southampton Terminus.

An operation of this complexity, fitting the trains and their return workings into an already busy schedule and of course without the help of computers or digital printing must have been a substantial challenge. Locomotives and carriage sets had to be found and marshalled. Their arrival at departure points was tightly timetabled and the trains waiting to go into Waterloo were queued on the down Windsor local line. Their movements were under the control of a pilotman and the arrangements logged by relevant signal boxes. A paragraph in the arrangements document states: 'The last train allowed to proceed over the down Windsor local line prior to that line being brought into use for berthing purposes will be the 5.34am Waterloo to Windsor, by which the pilotman must travel from Waterloo to Loco Junction and the train must stop specially at the latter box to set him down.' There are then detailed safety instructions to signalmen, hand signallers and the pilotman to ensure safe movements of the trains on this section of track. Each train was instructed to proceed cautiously, keep a sharp lookout and come to a stand clear of the preceding train: what was in effect permissive block working. Movements forward into Waterloo were also controlled by the pilotman with the aid of a hand signaller and considerable quantities of detonators.

WEDNESDAY, 19th, to FRIDAY, 21st May.

MAXIMUM LOADS OF MAIN LINE STEAM TRAINS ENTERING WATERLOO.

The maximum load of each Main Line Steam Train entering Waterloo Station is governed by the platform to which it is shown to run in this Notice. The maximum load for each platform concerned is shown below and must not be exceeded.

Platforms.	Load not to exceed.
5	9 bogie vehicles or equivalent and one engine.
6	11 bogie vehicles or equivalent and one engine.
7 and 8	10 bogie vehicles or equivalent and one engine.
9	12 bogie vehicles or equivalent and one engine.
10	12 bogie vehicles or equivalent and one engine (provided prior arrangements are made and agreed with the Station Master, Waterloo, 13 bogie vehicles or equivalent and one engine may be accepted).
11	12 bogie vehicles or equivalent and one engine (provided prior arrangements are made and agreed with the Station Master, Waterloo, 14 bogie vehicles or equivalent and one engine may be accepted).
12 and 13	12 bogie vehicles or equivalent and one engine (provided prior arrangements are made and agreed with the Station Master at Waterloo, 13 bogie vehicles or equivalent and one engine may be accepted).
14	12 bogie vehicles or equivalent and one engine.
15	9 bogie vehicles or equivalent and one engine.

All starting and attaching stations to note and advise all concerned that the instructions must be strictly adhered to in order to avoid serious delays owing to trains standing foul at Waterloo.

Respective platform capacities at Waterloo.

Special train details.

No. 146. SPECIAL TRAINS WILL CONVEY (Forward Journey).

Train No.	Name of Party.	No. of Passengers. 1st	No. of Passengers. 3rd	FROM Waterloo. a.m.	FROM Victoria. a.m.	Platform No.	TO Sou'ton Term. a.m.	TO Sou'ton Dock Gates. a.m.	TO Mill-brook Entrance. a.m.	TO P'mouth & S'sea. a.m.	TO P'mouth Hbr. a.m.	Name of Boat.
1	Nottingham Journal (ex G.W.R.).	—	450	(Basingstoke depart 6.0 a.m.)	—	—	6 45	—	—	—	—	I.O.W. S.P. Co.
2	Heelas (ex G.W.R.)	—	400	(Basingstoke depart 7.5 a.m.)	—	—	7 55	—	—	—	—	Princess Elizabeth.
45	O'Beirne	130	—	6 38	—	9	8 13	—	—	—	—	Lady Vagrant.
	Asiatic Petroleum Co.	60	—		—		—	—	—	—	—	Vulcan.
3	Lairdways & Reservations Ltd.	Mixed. 400		6 48	—	8	—	8 24	—	—	—	Essex Queen.
5	Lairdways & Reservations Ltd.	Mixed. 450		7 3	—	11	—	8 36	—	—	—	Queen of Southend.
6	British O. & C. Travel.	Mixed. 500		7 7	—	12	—	—	8 45	—	—	Queen of the Channel.
7	Pickfords	Mixed. 500		7 15	—	13	—	—	8 52	—	—	Crested Eagle.
8	Board of Trade	Mixed. 132 77		7 25	—	6	—	9 2	—	—	—	Dilwara. Lancashire. Lancashire passengers to be loaded in front of train.
	H. Clough	30		—	—		—	—	—	—	—	Private. Clough's party to be loaded in Dilwara portion.
9	Pickfords	Mixed. 500		7 30	—	14	—	—	9 13	—	—	Crested Eagle.
76	G.S.N. Co.	—	540	—	7 5	14	—	—	—	9 16	—	Medway Queen.
10	Sir H. Lunn	Mixed. 450		7 40	—	7	—	9 20	—	—	—	Glen Gower.
78	G.S.N. Co.	Mixed. 528		—	7 12	13	—	—	—	9 25	—	Royal Daffodil.
11	Sir H. Lunn	Mixed. 450		7 46	—	8	—	—	9 28	—	—	Glen Usk.
12	Frames	Mixed. 500		7 55	—	11	—	9 33	—	—	—	Britannia.
13	Polytechnic	Mixed. 500		8 0	—	6	—	9 39	—	—	—	Lorna Doone.
80	G.S.N. Co.	Mixed. 648		—	7 35	16	—	—	—	9 45	—	Royal Daffodil.
14	Sir H. Lunn	Mixed. 450		8 5	—	9	—	—	9 48	—	—	Brighton Queen.
82	Whichello	—	400	—	7 45	14 (Front)	—	—	—	9 54	—	Queen of Kent.
15	Hickie Borman	400	—	8 12	—	10	—	9 57	—	—	—	Maid of Orleans.
83	Whichello	—	400	—	7 51	14 (Rear)	—	—	—	10 5	—	Queen of Kent.
16	J. Brown Co.	310	—	8 20	—	12	—	10 6	—	—	—	Medina.
	Anglo Iranian Oil Coy.	55	—		—		—	—	—	—	—	Romsey.

SOUTHERN RAILWAY

Royal Naval Review at Spithead

Thursday, 20th May, 1937   **Thursday, 20th May, 1937**

GREAT ASSEMBLY OF BRITISH AND FOREIGN WARSHIPS

The following Excursions will be made by the
"SOUTHSEA," "WHIPPINGHAM," "SANDOWN," etc.
(Weather and other circumstances permitting)

TO VIEW THE FLEET

(Duration of Cruises to View the Fleet about 2 hours)

FRIDAY, 14TH MAY	**From Portsmouth Harbour** 3.30 p.m., 4.30 p.m., 6.0 p.m. **From Southsea (Clarence) Pier** 3.45 p.m., 4.45 p.m., 6.15 p.m.
SATURDAY, 15TH MAY	**From Portsmouth Harbour** 10.0 a.m., 11.0 a.m., 1.0 p.m., 2.0 p.m., 4.0 p.m., 5.0 p.m. **From Southsea (South Parade) Pier** 10.30 a.m., 11.30 a.m., 1.30 p.m., 2.30 p.m., 4.30 p.m., 5.30 p.m.
SUNDAY, 16TH MAY	**From Portsmouth Harbour** 10.0 a.m., 11.0 a.m., 12.45 p.m., 2.15 p.m., 3.30 p.m., 4.30 p.m., 6.15 p.m. **From Southsea (Clarence) Pier** 10.15 a.m., 11.15 a.m., 1.0 p.m., 2.0 p.m., 3.45 p.m., 4.45 p.m., 6.30 p.m. **From Ryde Pier** 2.15 p.m., 4.30 p.m.
MONDAY, 17TH MAY	**From Portsmouth Harbour** 11.0 a.m., 2.0 p.m., 3.0 p.m., 4.0 p.m., 5.45 p.m. **From Southsea (South Parade) Pier.** 11.30 a.m., 1.0 p.m., 2.30 p.m., 3.30 p.m., 4.30 p.m., 6.15 p.m.
TUESDAY, 18TH MAY	**From Portsmouth Harbour** 10.30 a.m., 11.0 a.m., 3.45 p.m., 4.30 p.m., 6.15 p.m., **From Southsea (Clarence) Pier** 10.45 a.m., 11.15 a.m., 12 noon, 4.0 p.m., 4.45 p.m., 6.30 p.m. **From Ryde Pier** 12.45 p.m., 3 0 p.m., 5.0 p.m.
WEDNESDAY 19TH MAY	**From Portsmouth Harbour** 9.30 a.m., 11.0 a.m., 2.0 p.m., 3.0 p.m., 4.0 p.m., 5.0 p.m. **From Southsea (South Parade) Pier** 10.0 a.m., 11.30 a.m., 2.0 p.m., 2.30 p.m., 3.30 p.m., 4.30 p.m., 5.30 p.m.

TO WITNESS THE ROYAL NAVAL REVIEW

THURSDAY 20TH MAY	From Southsea (Clarence) Pier	12.30 p.m.	*"Duchess of Norfolk"*
	From Southsea (South Parade) Pier	12.30 p.m.	*"Shanklin"*
	From Ryde Pier	1. 0 p.m.	

TO WITNESS ILLUMINATION OF THE FLEET

THURSDAY 20TH MAY	From Southsea (Clarence) Pier	8.15 p.m.	*"Whippingham"*
	From Southsea (South Parade) Pier	8.30 p.m.	
	From Ryde Pier	8.45 p.m.	*"Shanklin"*

FARES, including Pier Tolls, (No Half-fare for Children) :—

To View the Fleet	**3s. 0d.**
To Witness Naval Review	**7s. 6d.**
To Witness Illumination of Fleet	**3s. 6d.**

The number allowed on each steamer will be strictly limited, and passengers must embark at the Pier printed on the ticket.

Refreshments on board the Steamers at Tariff Prices.   Luncheon Cartons will also be obtainable on the "Duchess of Norfolk" and "Shanklin" on the Naval Review trip, price 1s. 6d. per carton.

CONDITIONS UPON WHICH THESE TICKETS ARE ISSUED.
These Tickets are issued subject to the conditions published in the Company's Time Tables and Notices and in the Railway Companies' "Book of Regulations relating to Traffic by Passenger Train or other similar service," and to the following special conditions:—
1. Neither the holder nor any other person shall have any right of action against the Company, or any other company or person owning, working or using any railway, vehicles, vessels, or premises (whether jointly with the Company or otherwise) upon which such tickets may be available in respect of (a) injury (fatal or otherwise), loss, damage or delay, however caused, or (b) loss of or damage or delay to property, however caused.
2. No luggage allowed except small handbags, luncheon baskets, or other small articles intended for the passenger's personal use during the day.

Waterloo Station, S.E.1   April, 1937   H. A. WALKER, General Manager

M. 18,035 2275—10   BARRELL, PORTSMOUTH & SOUTHAMPTON.

A separate notice contains details of 'carriage workings' for Waterloo, including newspaper trains and milk churn empties. A daunting array of train make up and times of movement from Clapham Yard or elsewhere is given, combining the additional movements into the regular timetable, but so comprehensive was the planning, and so well versed in organising this operation was the railway that very few regular workings are marked 'will not run'. No mention is made of light engine movements in the documents that I have but 65 special workings would also require 65 empty stock movements. There would then be 130 extra light locomotive movements: 65 train engines from Nine Elms and 65 released pilot locomotives that delivered the empty stock. A further complication is that the platforms at the termini were not of equal length. Stated capacities in the Carriage Working Notice at this time range from a normal capacity of 12 bogie vehicles plus engine to 9 bogies plus engine. The wrong train in a short platform would be an unwelcome complication!

SR Ships

Naturally, the Southern Railway's own vessels played a major part in the event. The ferry services would have been reduced and even suspended during the review itself – there was good money to be made running an excursion – especially if you could pre-book a few hundred people on both a ship and special train!

From the local area the Southern used the following ships which are all listed in association with the trains: *Southsea* (train 92, 570 passengers), *Sandown* (trains 96 and 40, 1,076 passengers), *Portsdown* (train 93, 350 passengers), *Whippingham* (train 94, 570 passengers), *Merstone* (train 91, 375 passengers plus 125 joining at Portsmouth), *Freshwater* (passengers from Brockenhurst and Lymington Pier), *Duchess of Norfolk* (142 passengers from Worthing and Seaford) and *Ryde* (train 95, 100 passengers). PS *Ryde* and PS *Sandown* would have been the pride of the SR fleet. *Sandown* was only three years old and *Ryde* had

entered service a matter of a few weeks before the event. *Sandown* is noted with provision for 'a party of 220 overseas scouts, to be placed in the front of the train', although surprisingly, *Ryde* has only 100 train passengers capacity booked. Other people must have been coming in by other means.

From Dover and Folkestone they brought in *Canterbury* (train 30, 375 passengers) and *Maid of Orleans* (train 15, 400 passengers). From the Southampton services: *Dinard* (train 26, 321 passengers), *Brittany* (train 27, 324 passengers), *Isle of Guernsey* (train 17, 330 passengers), *Isle of Jersey* (train 19, 600 passengers) and *Isle of Sark* (train 22, 450 passengers). *Brittany* was allocated to a party booked for the Directors of the SR.

General Steam Navigation

By this time the New Medway Steam Packet Co (NMSPCo) was part of the General Steam Navigation Co (GSN) and ships from both fleets, based on the Thames and Medway, ran excursions. The GSN supplied *Crested Eagle* (trains 7 and 9, 1,000 passengers), *Golden Eagle* (trains 89 and 90, 1000 passengers) and *Royal Eagle* (trains 35 and 36, 1,200 passengers). From the New Medway fleet came *Queen of the Channel* (trains 6 and 42, 850 passengers), *Medway Queen* (train 76, 540 passengers), *Queen of Kent* (trains 82 and 83, 800 passengers), *Queen of Thanet* (train 34, 370 passengers), *City of Rochester* (train 22, 200 passengers), *Queen of Southend* (train 5, 450 passengers), *Essex Queen* (train 3, 400 passengers) and *Royal Daffodil* (trains 78, 80 and 41, 1, 576 passengers).

P&A Campbell

P&A Campbell was another well-known excursion operator operating from Bristol and Weymouth. They sent *Glen Gower* (trains 10 and 43, 900 passengers), *Glen Usk* (train 11, 450 passengers), *Britannia* (train 12, 500 passengers) and *Brighton Queen* (train 14, 450 passengers).

PS *Medway Queen* as she was in the 1930s.

Red Funnel

The Red Funnel fleet from Southampton was certainly not going to be left out. Their ships listed are *Princess Elizabeth* (train 2, 400 passengers), *Balmoral* (train 22, 250 passengers), *Lorna Doone* (train 13, 500 passengers) and *Medina* (train 16, 310 passengers)

Other companies came from varying distances and, of course, ships actually involved in the Review often took passengers or pre-booked guests. Some trains connected with these ships or with tenders to ferry people out to them. The latter included P&O's 23,000-ton liner RMS *Strathmore* whose tender connected with an Admiralty party of 100 on train 20 from Waterloo. The *Cambria* from the railway-operated Holyhead services took 465 passengers from train 18, also from Waterloo.

The return journeys began from 8.42 pm from Portsmouth Harbour station and continued through the night until the last ones left Southampton Docks early on the Friday afternoon. Passengers would have been arriving back in London at all hours and throughout the following day providing rich pickings for the taxi drivers no doubt. This traffic, too, would have generated its own toll of empty stock workings and light engine movements.

It is interesting how the subsequent histories of some of the ships involved are intertwined. Vessels were bought and sold from one fleet to another and during World War 2 many (perhaps most) of these former passenger vessels were requisitioned and used as naval vessels, mostly as minesweepers at first and later in more diverse roles. Many were also involved in Operation 'Dynamo', the evacuation from Dunkirk with some being lost at that time. *Medway Queen* and several of her fleet mates were used for minesweeping as were the SR paddlers. *Sandown* and *Ryde* were both at Dover in the 10th Flotilla with *Medway Queen* in 1940. *Sandown* and *Medway Queen* went to Dunkirk although for some reason *Ryde* did not. From August 1940 *Medway Queen* served in the 8th M/S Flotilla with *Glen Gower*, *Glen Usk* and *Southsea*. HMS *Southsea* was mined and lost on 16 February 1941. After the war they went their separate ways, many meeting again in 1953 for another Spithead Review and then in the early 1970s PS *Ryde* joined *Medway Queen* on the Isle of Wight as the 'Ryde Queen Boatel'. *Queen of Kent* and *Queen of Thanet* were actually built as minesweepers for World War 1 (HMS *Atherstone* and HMS *Melton* respectively) and were converted to excursion

Their Majesties at the 1937 review. The *Southern Railway Magazine* for June 1937 (p202) refers to the review and also speaks of the 'The busiest fortnight ever' (for the SR), having commenced with the Coronation and terminating with the Spithead review. Two additional images accompany the article. In similar fashion, the *SRM* for July/August 1942 carries a general article by Frank E. Box on the subject of Royal Train journeys. This includes an illustration of one of the return review specials passing Haslemere on 21 May 1937 behind a 'T9'.

Published under the Authority of the Portsmouth Navy Week Committee

CORONATION REVIEW of the FLEET • SPITHEAD • 20TH MAY 1937. SOUVENIR PROGRAMME — • • — PRICE SIXPENCE.

ships for the NMSPCo in the 1920s. In 1939 they were requisitioned and converted again for their original purpose and then, after the war, went back into the excursion trade and were later sold on to Red Funnel where they would meet up with other war service survivors. Their post-war careers were brief, however, and both were scrapped in the early 1950s.

PS *Medway Queen* took a more formal part in the 1953 Coronation Review for Queen Elizabeth II – see *Southern Way* No 15. She is now berthed at Gillingham Pier in Kent and normally open to visitors on Saturdays. The lower aft saloon has been fitted as a display space and for the autumn of 2017 contains the story of the ship's appearances at the 1937 and 1953 Spithead Reviews. Disabled access to the ship may be restricted by the tides and below decks requires the use of short flights of stairs, but no ladders. Toilets are available on shore and Visitor Centre access is via ramps. Admission charge is £5 (for an annual ticket) per adult to go on board *Medway Queen*. Accompanied children under 16 have free admission. More details, terms and conditions at: www.medwayqueen.co.uk. (Readers who have access to the internet and 'YouTube' might care to click on to https://www.youtube.com/watch?v=-hYIGte7fBs , this is the hilarious BBC broadcast by Lt-Cdr Woodrooffe attempting to describe the 1937 Spithead Review. The poor man had, shall we say 'likely spent too much time in the wardroom beforehand'. They had to cut him off after about four minutes completely drunk. (With grateful thanks to Nick Grant for the information.)

(All images are from the Richard Halton collection unless otherwise stated.)

Right: **PS *Sandown* in later years, seen at Portsmouth Harbour station.** *Medway Queen Preservation Society collection*

Below: **PS *Ryde Queen*, recorded on 1 June 1985.**

Rebuilt
The Letters and Comments Pages

We start this issue's notes with a piece from Stuart Hicks: 'Kevin – your author for the SR article brought back all sorts of memories of my younger days living on the South Western division at New Malden and Walton on Thames in the 1960s and 1970s. He is, though, slightly incorrect on some of the details of the 1967 Bournemouth line stock.

'The 4REP units had a trailer brake first (not second) and the 4TC units each contained a trailer first (not a composite), as indeed did the 3TCs after strengthening.

'The 4VEP units had driving trailer composites at each end (not trailer composites), and one of the intermediate vehicles was a motor brake second with a large guards van. The luggage capacity of the latter was reduced in size at later rebuilding.

'None of these units started life with full yellow ends – they were basically all over blue with cast BR logos and a small yellow warning panel. Subsequently there were many changes to follow including all over yellow ends and the introduction of blue/grey livery. Finally the 1990 change was to NetworkSouthEast (three capitals, not two).'

Now from Mark Brinton: 'In response to your request for locations of the various 'O2' class images in *SW38*, I can suggest the following:

W19 (p99) is at Brading hauling an up train to Ryde, c1930.

W21 (p100) is also at Brading and again on an up train, c1935.

W25 (p100) is at Ryde Pier Head with a Ventnor line train, c1935.

W17 (p100) is at Brading with an up train, c1935.

W14 (p101) is at Brading chalk siding, c1935.

W16 (p101) is at Brading with an up train, c1935.

W25 (p101) is at Newport, c1935.'

Motor brake second from a VEP unit seen here at the time of building at York. It was the luggage capacity of these specific coaches on the VEP sets that was later reduced by the provision of two extra seating bays. *John Wenyon*

A completed VEP unit, this one No 7793. This was one of 134 sets built between 1967 and 1974, the fleet having a service life of 38 years. *John Wenyon*

Mark understandably also asks, 'What happened to the 'W22' at Bembridge photo mentioned in the text?' Simple answer here, I forgot to include it! On the basis then of better late than never ...

Following on also from various other Isle of Wight items that have appeared in *SW*, Roger Simmonds has submitted what is a 'then and now' for Petticoat Lane crossing at Newport: 'This is Petticoat Lane Crossing in Newport on the Freshwater, Yarmouth & Newport Railway. Very rarely photographed, this is the only view I have come across. It was taken on 12 May 1919 by Ken Nunn. On the extreme left is the corner of the Crossing Keeper's House which still survives to this day although somewhat modernised, and now hides behind a high fence if you walk up the lane. Two of the SR concrete gate posts also survive.

'The house was referred to as a "Gatekeeper's Lodge" in the FYN Railway Minute Books. The Gatekeeper also operated the signals shown in the photo.

'Unfortunately there is a sad tale as on 20 June 1903 the lady gatekeeper was killed after being hit by a train as she tried to save her deaf pet dog from running in front of the engine. Driver Harry Dore did all he could, but was unable to stop his engine in time. Her bereaved husband (also employed by the railway) had lost one of his legs 20 years previously on the railway at Cowes ... Later in SR days the gates were demolished by an earlier than expected goods train working on 28 September 1924. The Driver was not blamed as it was quite foggy and the rails were greasy.' (References: Isle of Wight County Press Archives)

The missing 'W22' at Bembridge.
Dave Hammersley collection

Why a 'Merchant Navy' at this point – well, read on and all will be revealed. 21C1 *Channel Packet* likely in as-built condition and still with the imposing number and ownership plates. Driver visibility was later improved on the original engines by slanting the can windows to reduce glare. *Les Elsey*

We have also received several letters from Eric Youldon. The first of these deals with Jeremy Clarke's 'comprehensive' article on the Locomotive Exchanges. Eric comments on the early BR prefix letter and reminds us that the early BR letter prefix applied only to some engines for a period of about three months and indicated the former owning company. Smokebox plates proper started being applied as engines passed through works from April 1948 onwards. Eric continues: 'Regarding headboards in the exchanges, the ER produced a nice "Atlantic Coast express" board for their "A4". This was briefly mounted at Waterloo to *Mallard* – there is a photograph on p.116 in C. J. Allen's book on the Locomotive Exchanges. Unfortunately senior authority saw this and ordered removal on the grounds it prevented the top route headcode disc being displayed. The "A1" in the earlier 1925 exchange was un-named at the time, "Victor Wild" came a littler later,'

Eric also comments on his notes about the decision not to use 'Duchess' Pacifics on the Southern in the 1960s. The year this was contemplated was 1964, not 1963, and the problem at Southampton was Northam curve and not the tunnel leading to Southampton Central. Another issue was at Weymouth where the turntable was only just long enough to take the overall wheelbase of a 'Duchess' attached to a 'WD' tender, plus of course the issue of spares.

Eric: 'Turning now to p.57 of "Rebuilt" in *SW*38. Jeremy Clarke is in error where he claims that Maunsell employed Marshall valve gear for the inside cylinder of his "Z" class 0-8-0T. In fact a modified Walschaerts gear was used that involved two eccentrics on the inside crank axle. One of these was set at 90° to the inside crank for operating the expansion link and the other eccentric was in phase with the main crank to take the place of the usual crosshead link to the combination lever.

This provided the "lap and lead" movement.

'With Marshall gear, steam admission was by a piston valve in a conventional way, but exhaust was controlled by a separate slide valve below the cylinder. The "Z" class layout can be studied from the General Arrangement drawing in the book on the class from Irwell Press.'

Eric also writes as follows: 'One of the many attractions of *SW* is the readiness to include all things Bulleid – which is a commendable vice! But there is one feature that has been ignored (forgive me if I am wrong – *no, you are correct – Ed.*) namely the testimonial presented to Bulleid in 1966 and compiled by Driver E. Pistell of Salisbury. Eligible drivers from Exmouth Junction, Nine Elms, and Salisbury were invited to sign the claim that his Pacifics were at their best before rebuilding. Eighty men signed and many added their own comments. A selection of the latter appear in the book *Bulleid of the Southern* by H. A. V. Bulleid. These make for fascinating reading in which the appreciation of the original design shows through. The ease of driver preparation is quoted by virtue of the self-contained oil bath although we know the fitters held a different view. Hence there clearly were two sides to the story.

From *Bulleid of the Southern* (Ian Allan, 1977), '"The performance of the engines before modification can be summed up in one word – 'MAGNIFICENT'. "Having worked these engines before and after modification, I consider that in their original design, they were themselves sufficient testimonial to a very fine engineer." "I personally thought they were the 'Cassius Clay' of locomotives, the greatest thanks again to that great designer Mr. Bulleid." "When working a passenger train with a 'West Country' engine over the Great Western road to Plymouth, a Motor Engineer paid a compliment by saying that she ascended

'In full flight'. Bulleid No 35021 *New Zealand Line* in Shawford cutting (just south of the station of the same name) in charge of the 9.20am Weymouth to Waterloo, 31 August 1958. *Tony Molyneaux*

Dainton Incline (2 miles at 1 in 50) as if she was fitted with a Rolls-Royce engine." "These were most economical and one of the fastest that it was my pleasure to drive. But now in the later years of conversion they have become stifled in the front end, retarding their running."'

Some drivers aired their personal dislikes amongst the praise:

'"The finest engines that ever ran on rails, the Rolls of locomotion. I've raised many an eyebrow with this remark as you can well imagine. My only complaint – no bucket seat. I must say, to get the true value from these wonderful engines one had to be a driver by nature. I can quite understand your feelings, a 'West Country' Class 6 was found to be so good they made it a Class 7 then decided they were not economic. What bosh! Perhaps you will have another name. To my regret what's left in my opinion have been sabotaged. I've stated facts as I see them after a life time of railway service – 50 years." "Best in the original design … good all-round engines for all classes of work in the West Country … In the modified condition the outlook was better but the screw-reverser was harder work." "With all the praise for these engines, don't let us forget the snags at maintenance level. And undoubtedly the most expensive piece of machinery any railroad produced. This is no reflection on Mr. Bulleid but on the Management that

sanctioned their construction." "When they were maintained properly they were unbeatable, masters of the job and good riders, also the electric lighting was a boon!" "My son was a fitter at Exmouth Junction and said failure of non-return valves in the mechanical lubricators was a cause of excessive wear in the inside valve bushes, also ashes being drawn down the blast pipe while coasting on freight trains, so the valve would lose some of its travel and form a ridge against which a valve ring would break and hence the engine became out in its beats. Undoubtedly had Mr Bulleid remained with us some of the lubrication troubles would have been dealt with …' Properly maintained the engines were the best I ever rode on and I rode on all the main line types on the Interchange runs between Salisbury and Exeter. During tests with the `WCs' over the WR route as between Bristol and Truro with both freight and passenger trains, the WR Inspectors riding with me were astounded at the performance and boiler efficiency which was capable of maintaining the heaviest demands."'

Some drivers had a bit to say about the steam reversers: '"They were, in my opinion, one of the finest engines ever built; it is also true that there were one or two faults with them, for example the steam hydraulic reverser, which gave very little trouble if properly maintained; the look-out, yes, bad at times when the wind was blowing the wrong way. All the little faults, we somehow managed to get over; it was the very free running of these engines that was the secret, and if properly managed, they were masters of their jobs – when they were in their original design. When they were modified, the Walschaerts valve gear fitted, the very free running was gone! Had to almost steam them into stations – not the same engine by any means." "The steam reversers were prone to creep. The main reasons for this (especially on 'West Countries') was, in my opinion, incorrect operation of the lever control by persons not understanding the correct way to operate this reverser and, of course, coupled with lack of maintenance when trouble was developing. As is so often the case with new machinery and modifications, no instructions were printed or told to the loco staff on the correct method of using this reverser; it was found by trial and error!" "The hydraulic cylinder was often a source of trouble as regards to keeping it full, I've seen buckets of oil used on them daily, filling up on leaving shed, and filling again at say Plymouth or Salisbury for the return journey, and the thing useless each way often at that. Starting away with a train at a station was often difficult; they did not seem to take steam and one would have to build the steam chest to full boiler pressure when they would slip at a terrific speed, but this would

often do them good as they would often afterwards go away with ease. This I considered was caused by the valves being thrown out to their full distance in the spin and would then take steam better. Now for the rebuilds. The screw reverser in one go did away with almost all the trouble as the new gear was 100% perfect as possible to get, the blast on the fire was more even and consequently a saving on coal ... When an engine will tackle 17 corridor coaches from Salisbury to Exeter as I did, tho' only once, as a young driver on a Saturday prior to August Bank Holiday when traffic was very heavy, it is a good bit of machinery. This was done with a 'Merchant Navy' of course and prior to its being rebuilt but in good nick! Rebuilding of course robbed them of no power. Am sorry 1 cannot go all the way with you." "I preferred them all in their original design for free running, you could run miles on atomised steam in 15% cut-off, they were also much easier in preparation. The steam reverser gave no trouble when hydraulic washers were kept in good order and cylinders topped up." "They were in my opinion the finest loco ever built – with one exception which was really a bad one, the Driver's look-out window in hazy weather or heavy rain – you just had it, visibility nil. But on going into Shops, that was

And just to show we are hopefully not too biased against the Eastern section, from the footplate of an original 'squadron' on the 'Arrow' – as they might say at Stewarts Lane. *Ron Pocklington*

rectified ... I had three days learning the road from Exeter St Davids to Plymouth North Road on *King George V*, the one that went over to the States, and I am fully convinced that the 'West Country' or 'Merchant Navy' would have left the 'King' standing! I was all for the steam reverser in preference to the wheel which was a real manual job to notch up against steam. damn hard work." "The creep was not so much to do with the topping with oil as it was the passing of oil, the washers being worn so badly – there again, maintenance! I was once asked by a gent at Bude how I liked them and I told him about the inside big end and gear being taken out of our hands by the oil bath, and that it took a lot of oil, and that it was a wonderful job. He said it did not matter about a barrow of oil: and that we drivers found out when they were modified – they were the dirtiest job of oiling we had in our lives! Mr Bulleid's engine was the best I have driven or rode on.'"

Several drivers had something to say about speed, and about their regrets at the passing of steam: '"The finest and fastest locomotives I have ever driven. I am only sorry that an official attempt to break the existing steam locomotive record was not made; I should have loved to have had the opportunity, and I feel sure it could have been broken – that is, of course, before they were modified." "The pick of the bunch in my experience was 34043 which I had booked to me when I was working in the Ilfracombe passenger link. She was brand new at the time and, in the old loco men's saying, 'She would catch pigeons.'" "Both before and after modification the performance of this class of locomotive was marvellous. On one occasion with a load of seven bogies I started from Axminster and passed Whimple in 15min. One performance that is worth recalling is that of driver Hamilton. With a load of six bogies he started from Salisbury and passed Yeovil in 33min." "I have enclosed a running by me of the 'Atlantic Coast Express,' which was taken unknown to me." (The timings include passing Yeovil in 36min 20sec and passing Axminster in 54min, from Salisbury; engine No 35014, tare load 435 tons.) "Also when the paper train used to run non-stop from Salisbury to Exeter, I have done it in 1hr 15min, which I think speaks well of the free running of these engines." "In appreciation of the Pacifics which in my opinion could have beaten *Mallard's* record." "I am only too pleased to testify to the supreme qualities of Mr Bulleid's Pacifics. Those engines would outrun, and out pull any steam engine I have ever handled. My experience of steam engines is wide and varied, from the old L&SWR Sharp's and Adams' high-wheelers down to the last of the steam engines, including the famous *Mallard*. Now that I am retired I can tell you that the record put up by the *Mallard* has been broken – unofficial, of course – many times by these engines of Mr Bulleid. I would be speaking tongue in cheek if I didn't say that these engines had some drawbacks, notably poor lookout, and the steam reversing gear was often at fault, but overall they were the most capable engines I have ever handled."

'"The riding of the suspension under the footplate was immaculate to the other engines that had gone before it; there was also complete absence of axlebox knock with these

Away from steam and into the 1980s. Former Eastleigh driver Dave Darcy has kindly submitted this image of him at the head of the Chipman's weed-killing train at London Bridge hauled by two de-icer units. The unusual combination was due to the fact that locomotives were not then permitted over the Atlantic bridge, which was the required route for the working. The service had started from Victoria and would terminate shortly, a Class 33 coming on to the back end of the tanks whilst Dave then took the units to Selhurst before booking off duty. Although Eastleigh based, Dave had commenced his driving career at Victoria and consequently possessed considerable route knowledge.

engines running at all speeds. It is my firm opinion that this rebuilt machine lacks freedom in its running and due to this alteration these engines lack potency in power output, and both the riding and general axlebox and valve motion knock has deteriorated its performance." "When the 'West Country' class came to Exmouth Junction, Driver R. Dawe and myself had No 10, which was named *Sidmouth*, to ourselves, early and late turns of duty on the run Exeter to Ilfracombe, and what a grand and reliable engine to have had, and what a lovely ride. Everyone really admired those engines; what a great pity they were ever taken out of service."' (The original testimonies are lodged in the Library of the Institution of Mechanical Engineers.)

Finally, a letter from John Harvey (Editor of *Southern Notebook*.) 'In *SW*36, I'm not convinced that Mr Sayers-Leavy gets to the heart of the reasons for "Steam Heat Conservation" trials with A816. I wonder whether he has read Holcroft's first-hand account in *Locomotive Adventure* Vol 1 chapter 8? The point is that the potential savings were immense due to "steam heat conservation". Maunsell was cautious: he was not really interested in the theory, but asked for and got, a practical demonstration with measured results showing how much could be saved before agreeing to a railway locomotive trial. The savings amounted to 29%. Now, in 1913 (the only figures I have to hand) the combined locomotive fuel expenses for the LSWR, LBSCR and SECR amounted to £1,168 million, whilst wages amounted to £695,000 and the total steam locomotive running expenses came to £2,064 million. Adjusted to the early 1930s, these figures become £1,869 million for fuel, £1,112 million for wages and £3,302 total using the Bank of England calculator. In today's money, the 1913 figures have to be multiplied by a factor close to 100, ie a fuel cost of around £117 millions.

'The potential savings in today's money were therefore as much as £34 millions (today's money) and even if only a fraction of that had been realised then I contend that it was worth going after with a trial. Indeed, I believe that as the person responsible for the Southern Railway's coal account, Maunsell would have been negligent if he had not made a serious investigation of the possibilities. Yes, the costs of the additional auxiliaries, both in running expenses and maintenance, would eat into the savings, but the fact that those required were built into A816 and did not exceed loading gauge or axle loading showed that it was possible.

'The draughting fan was not big enough but that must have been capable of development and it seems to me to be a pity that the project was dropped. The mistake concerning the incorrect fitting of the impeller should not have happened, but what about the first of the GWR "56xx" class when they tried to move it under its own steam? (The drawing office forgot to incorporate a cross-head and slide bars for the valve rods so they bent under the imposed forces). Then there was one of a new class of Beyer-Garratt locos (I think it was) which, when driven for the first time the regulator was opened but the engine did not move. (There was a design error in the reversing gear so that one bogie tried to go forwards and the other backwards).

'I could make a number of other points, but I believe it was Hackworth who invented the blastpipe and whilst simple and effective, numerous issues associated with either poorly steaming locomotives on the one hand and substantial locomotive performance and efficiency losses on the other caused Engineers to scratch their heads over many years. Matching an effective and efficient blastpipe to the demands of the boiler to make steam was not simple. Perhaps Kylala, Chapelon, LeMaitre and Giesl were wrong, but I don't think so and I believe we should applaud all those Locomotive Engineers who took George Stephenson's ideas of the 1820s and developed them into machines suitable for powering our trains into the middle of the 20th Century.'

Two other 'Southern' experiments that were not perpetuated. The first is of the Drummond 4-2-2-0 'double-single' No 720, built at Nine Elms in 1920 and seen here in the process of being dismantled at Eastleigh on 23 April 1927. Seven years later it is the Marshall valve gear fitted 'N'. No 1850 is outside the front of Eastleigh works on 23 September 1934, no doubt following a test run. Although marginally more efficient than a standard member of the 'N' class on trial, the gear had a tendency to knock above 50mph and its fate was sealed when the right-hand side later disintegrated whilst working a Waterloo-bound train.

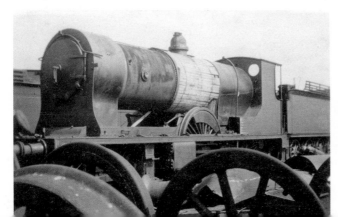

The Southern's Versatile 'Standard 5s'

Underneath a liberal coating of grime, green-liveried 73029 awaits the right away from Brockenhurst with a Waterloo service during the last year of SR steam in 1967.

In this feature Jeffery Grayer recalls the geographical distribution of the SR's complement of the useful BR Standard Class 5 4-6-0s.

Ubiquitous on all regions of BR, the 171 members of the '73xxx' Standard Class 5 4-6-0, represented one of the more successful designs from the Standard portfolio. All regions had examples on their books at one time or another and the SR was no exception having no less than 47 different members of the class allocated to them during their 17-year working lifetime which lasted from 1951 until 1968. Details of the SR's allocation and their withdrawal details are shown in Appendix 1.

A number of Standard Class 5s, which were the equivalent of the LMS 'Black 5', were to be allocated to the SR from new in 1955 and proved to be highly successful in handling both express passenger and loose-coupled freights. That they

continued until the end of steam on the SR in July 1967, and indeed to the end of steam on BR in August 1968, is a testament to the high regard in which they were held by railwaymen and to their usefulness and reliability in traffic.

The majority were constructed at Derby with the remainder produced by Doncaster Works. Designed by Riddles, the first locomotive entered traffic in April 1951 and immediately proved itself to be a success. They were paired with six different tenders ranging from the BR1 to the BR1F. On the SR the initial allocation was destined for the Kent Coast lines but when those routes were electrified many were transferred to work on the South Western section and so helped to displace older Southern types still in service.

Destined to have a far shorter working life than was originally intended, the first of the type to be withdrawn was No 73027 on 29 February 1964 from Swindon shed, after little more than 12 years' service, the final example, No 73069, lasting until August 1968 at Carnforth shed. The SR examples were allocated to just seven sheds during their stay on the region (see Appendix 2). At the beginning of 1966 the SR still had 31 Standard Class 5s on their books. One year later this was reduced to 18, with just 10 examples lasting until the end of steam on 9 July 1967. Thirty Class 5s were provided with Caprotti valve gear and poppet valves although none of these was allocated to the SR. (One example was noted on Eastleigh shed in the mid 1960s but this had been sent for works repair from the LMR.)

Five examples are preserved including two of the class which worked on the SR* – No 73050 on the Nene Valley Railway, No 73082 *Camelot* on the Bluebell Railway, No 73096 on the Mid Hants Railway, No 73129, a Caprotti valve gear variant, at the Midland Railway Centre Butterley and finally No 73156 currently undergoing restoration at Loughborough on the Great Central Railway. No 73129 along with 71000 *Duke of Gloucester* are the only two BR locomotives with Caprotti valve gear that remain today. (*Nos 73050 and 73082 are ex Southern Region engines.)

The decrepit Weymouth coaling stage plays host to No 73117, formerly 'Vivien', which lasted in traffic until March 1967.

Lit by a low-lying sun an unkempt No 73117 again, in a condition so typical of the last months of steam, sits in light steam outside Eastleigh shed. The name 'Vivien' was formerly carried by Urie N15 No 30478, withdrawn in 1957.

Against the backdrop of Southampton Central's impressive signal gantry, the BR1 tender of No 73020 is replenished during a station stop en route to Bournemouth in 1966. One can almost smell the sunlit-faded moquette of the compartment of the green Bulleid carriage at the head of the rake.

In a line up of four Standard classes outside Eastleigh shed in January 1967, No 73171, the last of the class numerically, lies devoid of coupling rods ready for onward towing to the scrapyard, in this case Cashmore's of Newport, where it was despatched in March 1967 after a short working life of just 9½ years.

The rusting wheel rims testify to the fact that No 73016 has been dumped for some time at the rear of Weymouth shed following withdrawal in December 1966.

The bare minimum of cleaning has revealed the identity of locomotive No 73037, done no doubt for crew recognition purposes, seen outside Eastleigh shed. This engine was active into the final week of steam on the SR, being noted on the 17.16 Southampton–Bournemouth service on 3 July 1967.

The SR had none of the Caprotti valve gear examples and No 73125, which was captured at Patricroft shed, is one of several that lasted until a few weeks before the end of BR steam in August 1968. Behind is No 73050, one of the five members of the class which did make it into preservation.

Appendix 1. Standard Class 5s at one Time Allocated to SR Sheds

No	Withdrawn	Storage location
73002	3/67	Weymouth
73016	12/66	Weymouth
73017	10/64	Weymouth/Eastleigh
73018	7/67	Weymouth
73020	7/67	Weymouth/Salisbury
73022	4/67	Salisbury
73029	7/67	Salisbury
73037	7/67	Salisbury
73041	6/65	Guildford/Eastleigh
73042	8/65	Salisbury
73043	7/67	Salisbury
73046	9/64	Eastleigh
73047	12/64	Bath Green Park
73049	3/65	Oxford
73050	6/68	Patricroft
73051	8/65	Bath Green Park
73052	12/64	Bath Green Park
73065	7/67	Salisbury
73073**	10/67	Patricroft
73074	9/64	Eastleigh
73080* *Merlin*	12/66	Weymouth
73081* *Excalibur*	7/66	Guildford
73082* *Camelot*	6/66	Eastleigh (Preserved)
73083* *Pendragon*	9/66	Nine Elms
73084* *Tintagel*	12/65	Nine Elms/Salisbury
73085* *Melisande*	7/67	Salisbury
73086* *The Green Knight*	10/66	Eastleigh
73087* *Linette*	10/66	Guildford/ Nine Elms
73088* *Joyous Guard*	10/66	Eastleigh /Salisbury
73089* *Maid of Astolat*	9/66	Eastleigh /Salisbury
73092	7/67	Weymouth
73093	7/67	Salisbury
73110* *The Red Knight*	1/67	Nine Elms
73111* *King Uther*	9/65	Eastleigh
73112* *Morgan Le Fay*	6/65	Nine Elms
73113* *Lyonesse*	1/67	Eastleigh
73114* *Etarre*	6/66	Weymouth
73115* *King Pellinore*	3/67	Eastleigh/Salisbury
73116* *Iseult*	11/64	Eastleigh
73117* *Vivien*	3/67	Eastleigh
73118* *King Leodegrance*	7/67	Salisbury
73119* *Elaine*	3/67	Nine Elms/ Salisbury
73155	7/67	Salisbury
73167***	8/65	Shrewsbury
73168	12/65	Basingstoke/ Eastleigh
73169	10/66	Eastleigh
73170	6/66	Weymouth
73171	10/66	Eastleigh

*Named between 1959–1961 after withdrawn 'King Arthur' class locomotives and known as the 'Standard Arthurs'.
**Allocated to 71G from 4/55 to 7/55
***Allocated to 70B from 9/63–8/64

No 73110 *The Red Knight* runs past Radipole Lake on the approaches to Weymouth past well filled goods sidings in the winter of 1966 with a local service from Bournemouth. The locomotive was withdrawn in January the following year.

No 73029 runs into Southampton Central light engine past the former power station seen on the right of this view. The old power station which stood on the present Toys-R-Us site at Western Esplanade was a local landmark and for decades was the first thing passengers saw when they arrived by train at Central station. Electricity generation ceased in 1972 when Fawley power station came on stream but the building remained, gradually being demolished over the following few years with the chimneys not disappearing until 1975.

Appendix 2. SR MPDs in the Shed Code Range 70A–75G to Which Standard Class 5s Were Allocated

An unidentified member of the class runs into Southampton Central with a Bournemouth service affording a closer view of the former power station on the right.

Code	Shed	No of different examples allocated (1955–1967)
71G	Bath Green Park (Recoded 82F in 2/58)	9
71A	Eastleigh (Recoded 70D in 9/63)	31
70B	Feltham	13
70C	Guildford	20
70A	Nine Elms	30
73A	Stewarts Lane (Recoded 75D in 6/62)	10
71G	Weymouth (Recoded 70G in 9/63)	13

Exmouth Junction shed was recoded from 72A to 83D in 9/63 but did not receive its first allocation of five Standard Class 5s, until after recoding. These were:

	from	until
73030	10/63	9/64
73044	10/63	1/65
73161	9/63	1/65
73162	9/63	1/65
73166	10/63	9/64

Yeovil Town shed was recoded 83E in 9/63 but did not receive its first allocation, of one Standard Class 5, until after recoding. This was:

	from	until
73166	9/64	6/65

New Information on the 'EDs'
(the Electro-Diesels)

'ED' and 'TC' units as finally produced. The train is a Bournemouth–Waterloo 'fast – hence the '91' headcode – and likely in charge of the 'ED' as a REP set was not available. Taken between Winchester and Basingstoke around the time of the Bournemouth electrification in 1967.

A recent visit to the National Archives at Kew relative to some totally unrelated research, found me searching through some BR papers dated 13 December 1956 (AN/97/296). These reveal an interesting report on the electro-diesel concept then under consideration for the Southern Region. So on the basis that information gained should be shared …

'Memorandum to the Technical Development Research Committee on the Electro-Diesel Locomotive.

This paper has been prepared at the request of the Chairman to enable the present position with respect to the electro-diesel type of locomotive to be ventilated. It is shown that the special features of the Southern Region system rather lend themselves to the conception of this special type of locomotive and that considerable thought has been given to its possibilities over a period of some 10 years. Design projects have been worked out both in the Drawing Offices of the Southern Region and by The English Electric Company, and authority was sought (without success) for building prototype locomotives by the former Chief Electrical Engineer of the Railway Executive (R.E. Memo. M.2695 of 5/6/50).

'The matter has recently been mentioned again in connection with the diesel electric multiple unit trains for the Hastings services and the purpose of this paper is to enable the Committee to be given sufficient information to show why it is not considered a practical proposition to devote development work to this special variation of the diesel electric technique at present.

'The main objections are economic, since costs are not particularly attractive if similar performance is required with both forms of propulsion. There is, however, added technical complexity in the case of d.c. systems since here the motors would be called upon to receive current via sharply contrasting methods of control.

'The annual costs which vary as between diesel electric and electric propulsion can be divided into three parts:

1. Capital charges

2. Maintenance costs

3. Operating costs (principally fuel)

'To enable the diesel electric units to use a conductor rail feed, fairly substantial additions would be required to the equipment and therefore to its cost. A short estimate would be about 10%.

'The maintenance costs of the diesel engine might be reduced, although this is doubtful in view of the greater number of more or less cold starts to which the engine would be subjected. The maintenance costs of the rest of the equipment would certainly be greater because there would be more of it.

'The operating costs would probably not be very different because the cost of the principal element, fuel, would be about the same.

'As experience is gained with the new types of diesel engine now being produced it is possible that the disadvantages mentioned above can be reduced, and it may well be possible within a reasonable time to produce something which will on the one hand satisfy the operating needs and on the other will not be so heavily equipped as to be ruled out economically.

'I propose to have this matter reviewed at regular intervals since the application of the electro-diesel design must not necessarily be regarded as exclusive to third rail d.c. electrification systems. The possibilities of its use on overhead lino systems must also be considered, particularly with a.c. where the presence of the transformer may enable a diesel driven a.c. generator to be used with the same control system.

'The attached appendix gives a more detailed exposition of the problems

S. B. Warder, Chief Electrical Engineer.'

The file then continues on the same basic topic but apparently without the referred to appendix being present. 'Alternatively it is possible to install a complete diesel electric generator set but it will be appreciated that this increases the capital cost and space required. On conventional d. c. stock, however, a variable supply voltage is not readily obtainable and the speed control of the motors is carried out by switching resistances in series with traction motors. There is therefore a fundamental difference in principles of control which complicates the problem of applying auxiliary diesel power. The existing Southern Region Co-Co electric locomotives are equipped with two motor generator sets of the type described, each of about 750 H.P., giving a total locomotive output of some 1,500 H.P. This power was found more than adequate for the heaviest freight trains operated and it was considered that a medium power unit of about half the power of the Co-Co locomotive might have found acceptance for operating pick-up freight trains and light passenger traffic in the electrified area. It was therefore proposed to build a locomotive basically similar to the existing Southern Region electric locomotives but with one motor generator set removed and the space this made

available occupied by a diesel power unit. Three designs based on this conception were considered.'

This followed by various paragraphs lettered/numbered 'A–C' and '3–5'. There did not appear to be any pages missing.

'**(a) 1,250 H.P. electric + 440 H.P. diesel locomotive**. At the time this matter was under consideration, the design of the 2,500 H.P. electric locomotive now proposed for the Southern Region Eastern and Central Section electrification was also being developed. It was then intended that these locomotives should have two motor generator sets each of 1,250 H.P. (the locomotives to be built will in fact have one 2,500 H.P. motor generator set.)

'Since it was believed that a 1,250 H.P. set would have to be developed for the electric locomotive it was intended to use one of the 1,250 H.P. motor generator sets together with a 440 H.P. diesel electric generator set.

'This arrangement produced a general purpose locomotive providing 1,250 H.P. with a maximum speed of 72 m.p.h. for passenger and freight work on electrified lines and 440 H.P. with a maximum speed of 25 m.p.h. for shunting in non-electrified yards.

'This locomotive was basically a motor generator electric locomotive capable of dealing with freight train loadings of up to 800 tons on the electrified lines, and as soon as it entered yards and sidings not equipped with the third rail it would have made use of its diesel engine and generator to give a performance comparable to that of the normal diesel electric shunting locomotive. To obtain the maximum utilisation, the locomotive could also have been used for relief and excursion passenger trains hauling 350 tons at 63 m.p.h. on the level, working as a straight electric locomotive, and there was a suggestion that if the diesel unit could be brought into the circuit the locomotive could be made capable of hauling 450 tons at 72 m.p.h. As the design was chiefly included for freight working and Summer passenger working, carriage heating equipment was not included. Since that time the opinion has been held that the technical problems involved in protecting the generator when connected in series with the conductor rail supply were sufficiently complex to make this particular project unattractive.

'**(b) 800 H.P. electric + 250 H.P. diesel locomotive.** The same principle was also applied in the design of a smaller locomotive having a motor generator set of the type used in the existing Southern Region electric locomotives. This proposal produced a Bo-Bo locomotive weighing about 65 tons (i.e. an axle load of about 16.25 tons) with a single cab and arranged for multiple unit operation. The use of the existing design of motor generator set avoided additional development charges and again provided a relatively simple solution to the problem of suitable auxiliary power for shunting movements away from electrified tracks.

'The suggested method was to provide a small high speed lightweight diesel engine of 250 H.P. which could be coupled with the motor generator shaft when required. Operated electrically the locomotive would have had a starting tractive effort of some 24,000 lb. which could have been maintained up about 24 m.p.h. and could have hauled a 500 ton freight train at 34.5 m.p.h. or a seven coach passenger train at 54 m.p.h. on the level.

'Operating on the diesel engine the same starting tractive effort would have fallen away to 3,800 lb. at 20 m.p.h.

'(c) 800 H.P. electric and 800 H.P. diesel engine. This design was evolved following discussions with the Operating Department Southern Region, who did not favour the previous designs on the ground that the provision of limited diesel power was not worthwhile since it would result in uneconomical rostering of the locomotive, the amount of work available for it at this limited. output being very small.

'As a result of the operating requirement that the locomotive should be capable of approximately the same performance on and off the conductor rail, this design envisaged the use of an 800 H.P. English Electric "Deltic" engine coupled to the existing design of motor generator set through a magnetic clutch. With this arrangement of power unit, it was estimated that a Bo-Bo locomotive weighing about 70 t0ns could produce the same performance whether working from the conductor rail or from the diesel auxiliary, namely a maximum speed of 75 m.p.h. with ability to haul a 245 ton, passenger train or a 500 ton freight train on the level at 54 m.p.h. or 32.4 m.p.h. respectively.

'It should be remembered that the types mentioned in (a) and (b) above would be suitable for a completely electrified system where only sidings have been left unwired, whereas the type described under (c) is more essentially for an electrified system still retaining non-electrified. branch lines. The locomotive would then be able to run through one to another without change of loads.

Below and overleaf: **On the basis that we know what an 'ED' looks like, something else electric to conjure with. It shows the two locomotives operated by British Electricity and in use at Southampton Power Station. That lettered is No 3, built by Messrs Greenwood and Batley as their works No 1620 of 1939. The second is No 2, from Messrs Baguley, works No 2048 of 1931. More information on this industrial line may be found on pages 137-9 of** *Southampton's Railways* **by Bert Moody, published Kingfisher, and page 63 of** *The Industrial Railways of Southern England* **published by the Industrial Railway Society. Both images were taken on 3 August 1950 by John Bailey.**

'3. Electro-Diesel Locomotive on 1500v D.C. If the principle of the electro-diesel locomotive can be applied on the Southern Region there would appear to be corresponding justification for its application elsewhere on the 1500v D.C. overhead system. Accordingly consideration was given to the possibility of utilising the electro-diesel locomotive on the Manchester/Sheffield/Wath line. The 1500v locomotives, however, do not rely on the motor generator form of operation and there is no space available in the Bo-Bo type of locomotive to install a diesel generator set, and consequently it would be necessary to build a larger unit of the Co-Co type. This would make the electro-diesel type of unit much more expensive than its straight electric counterpart, possibly 25% more, whereas the third rail locomotives of the Southern Region, which must of necessity be provided with motor generators, are already more costly machines so that the difference in cost between the straight electric and electro-diesel engine design is not so pronounced.

'Again, the predominance of freight traffic on the Northern lines requires a great many more locomotives than would be necessary on the Southern, all of which would have to be specially equipped with diesel engines, and consequently the incentive for the adoption of this principle, namely the saving in cost of wiring in yards, would be largely destroyed. This is not the case on the Southern Region where the predominating traffic is passenger, operated by multiple unit trains, and very little freight working.

'4. Electro-Diesel Locomotives on A.C. systems. Detailed consideration of the use of electro-diesel locomotives on the a.c. system have not yet been made but the remarks above dealing with the cost of application to 1500v d. c. systems are broadly applicable.

'On the technical side, however, the rectifier a.c. locomotive is essentially a variable voltage machine and there should be no technical difficulty in applying auxiliary diesel power wherever an economic case can be made out.

'5. Conclusion. The chief source of application for electro-diesel locomotives is where traffic on and off electrified lines, such as occurs for pick up freight trains, is relatively small and where a large number of individual installations of wiring would otherwise be necessary. These conditions exist on the Southern Region to a much greater extent than in other regions.

'In addition, the special type of electric locomotive necessary for the third rail system of the Southern Region is not so costly to adapt to the electro-diesel principle as straight electric locomotives designed to work off overhead contact wire systems.

'The electro-diesel locomotive will, however, always be heavier a priority than an electric locomotive of equal horsepower, and the possible effects on the diesel set of running as an electric locomotive for long periods with the engine and generator stationary are not known.

The Uckfield Line

Alan Elliott
(Introduced by the Editor)

Likely one of Alan's prized finds, Uckfield's second railway station, built in 1868 and replaced in 1901. Alan notes, 'The footbridge does not appear on maps of 1873 – so when was it added?' There was no accommodation provided for the station master and who consequently lived in new town. Those incumbents in-post in the 19th century were:

1869 George William Humphrey

1888 William Reeves

1892 James Thomas Gladwin

1899 Henry Roach.

(The dates shown are when the respective names first appeared in local directories and are not necessarily the year of appointment.) No names are given for the men shown in the image.

In 1988 the late Alan Elliott had his seminal work on the Cuckoo Line published by Wild Swan. With Alan's book now long out of print, in 2016 the present author produced a pictorial work on the same route, not intended in any way to usurp Alan's book but instead to present some additional illustrations of what was an iconic railway.

I never met Alan, although I know our paths had crossed as his name was mentioned by the doubtable Reg Randell at the old Plan Arch at Waterloo. I suspect also like many who spend years researching and preparing a book on a specific line (or subject), when it eventually goes off to the publisher there is an unexpected void, almost a 'what do I do next?' situation.

SOUTHERN RAILWAY, UCKFIELD STATION STAFF 1921.

Uckfield station staff 1924. Station Master W. D. Lee is seated in the front row. Others are not positively identified but second from the left may be E. Mitchell and second from the right A. Ager. The photograph was taken on the up platform with the seat specially positioned for the occasion.
Courtesy John and Mary Browning

Sometimes this can manifest in a new hobby or interest, or a time to catch up on all those chores temporarily left moribund whilst time had been spent in the research, collecting and eventual compilation of a manuscript. Digressing slightly, I recall some years ago meeting a man whose researches had become so intense they overwhelmed him and he eventually gave the lot away and turned instead to something totally unrelated to railways. That was not the case with Alan, for although his was a name I had certainly heard of and indeed wondered if there might have been another work pending, I never thought I would find out. That is until 2016 and a coincidental chat with a lady in the village nearby whose name was – Mrs Elliott. In the course of the discussion she mentioned something along the lines of 'What do you do?', I responded accordingly and which soon led to a meeting with Robert Elliott, one of the sons. From this I learned there was indeed some railway material but at this stage I was unsure if it would again relate to the Cuckoo Line, or was indeed a potential further text.

It transpired it was a bit of both – 1% Cuckoo and 99% other, and most of the other was clearly the start of another work, this time on the line between Tunbridge Wells West, through Uckfield to Lewes. Exactly how far Alan had progressed we cannot be certain as it is far from a complete work, but he does make reference as intending to major on both Tunbridge Wells West and Lewes and of course to cover the locations in-between.

Having through the kind offices of the Elliott family had access to the surviving text and illustrations gathered it is clear this was a 'work in progress' although Alan's methodical brain had already listed out his intended chapter headings as well as lists of images as well as archives and sources yet to be checked. Even so I suspect not all his material may have survived but we must indeed be grateful for what does. His projected chapters are referred to in hard copy but there is also mention of files held on discs and CD. The computer files were likely Amstrad type and are no longer around (remember the '8512' and '8256' Amstrad machines or am I showing my

We move forward now to 1927 and a more detailed staff view. Back row left to right: F. Stevens, F. Walder, R. (Bob) Johnson – booking clerk, F. Hunt – signalman, G. Browning – porter. Front row left to right: L. Pelling, A. Ager, Station Master W. D. Lee, R. Lissiter, E. Mitchell. This time the view was taken at the loading bay at the station end of the goods shed on a wintry day – leafless branches on the trees visible beyond the up canopy, plus the men have their hands in their pockets and are wearing heavy coats. *Courtesy John and Mary Browning*

age – again?). But we must not dwell on what may have gone and instead concentrate on what survives, which includes that what follows on the early days of the Uckfield line as well as a set of delightful images of Uckfield. This material is now presented and also used where possible in Alan's own words. (Later issues of *SW* will include further extracts but as stated above, do not expect a complete work, as the remainder is again extracts.)

Had it been completed Alan's work would no doubt have been a definitive work; it may not have survived in full but what there is that remains is still remarkable.

The Uckfield Branch 1857–1868

The beginnings of the Uckfield branch came in 1857 when an independent company, the Lewes & Uckfield Railway, obtained powers to build a branch off the Keymer loop to link with the market town of Uckfield. This line opened in 1858 and for the next 10 years it operated as a self-contained branch.

The first Board Meeting of the new company was held in its office at 17, High Street, Lewes, on 28 July 1857, when the following directors were present:

John Ellman, Chairman

Alexander Donovan, Deputy Chairman

Robet Willis Blencowe

George Charles Dalbiac

Burwood Godlee

Edward Monk

William Kenward the younger

John Smith was appointed as Secretary and Bookkeeper and it was agreed that R. Jacombe-Hood, the Resident Engineer of the LBSCR, should be the Engineer. The Contractor was to be George Wythes.

The first Ordinary General Meeting of shareholders took place in the same office one month later, on 26 August 1857, and the following were present:

Robert Willis Blencowe, Director – in The Chair

Alexander Donovan, Director

George Charles Dalbiac, Director

John Ellman, Director

Sir Charles William Blunt, Bt

Rev. Charles Gaunt

John George Dodson, MP

William Kenwad Snr, Director

John Newnham

John Blaker, Auditor

Richard Henry Billiter

Arthur Rennie Briggs

Richard Peters Rickman, Auditor

It was resolved that the Secretary Bookkeeper should receive an annual salary of £100. Messrs Blaker and Rickman were appointed as Auditors at an annual fee of £10 each and it was resolved also that the directors should each receive £100 per annum.

Six months later, at the second Ordinary General meeting in February 1858, it was reported that work had commenced in November 1857, and that the contractor expected to complete the work in the Autumn. The Engineer was able to report that five of the seven route miles had been fenced in and two miles had been completed to formation ready for ballasting. A further three quarters of a mile had already been ballasted and construction of the bridge across the River Ouse was expected to start in a few days. About 300 men, 90 wagons and 40 horses were employed. LBSCR locomotives numbered 54, 57 and 59, all originally Hackworth singles, were also used in the construction of the line.

It was announced at the third Ordinary General Meeting on 24 August 1858 that the line was expected to open a few weeks later at the end of September. There were problems, however, and at the Board Meeting held on 28 September it was reported that Captain Tyler, RE, of the Board of Trade, had inspected the line on the previous day and had postponed the opening for one month. This was mainly because of the lack of a large turntable at Uckfield but an undertaking on the method of working was also required:

'... either that one engine in steam or two or more when coupled together and forming part of a train should ever be upon the single line or upon defined portions thereof at one and the same time, or that a train staff should be employed for the whole line or defined portions thereof as shown in the note appended to the letter of Capt. Gratton of the 7th September, 1858.'

At their meeting on 5 October 1858, it was reported to the Board that there had been a meeting with Captain Gratton, RE, at the Board of Trade and, subject to the use of tank engines only and the giving of the undertaking of the method of working, the line could open forthwith. A letter was sent to the Directors of the LBSCR stating these conditions.

Congratulations were offered at the fourth Ordinary General Meeting on 22 February 1859, when it was reported that the line had opened on 18 October 1858, and that traffic had already developed highly satisfactorily. It was also reported that the LBSCR had introduced a Bill to enable them to purchase the company.

As nearly as possible all business had been brought to a close, ready for the transfer of the company to the LBSCR, by the time of the fifth Ordinary General Meeting which took place on 30 August 1859. The LBSCR Bill received Royal Assent on 1 August 1859.

The sixth and final Ordinary General Meeting was held on 29 February 1860, and this was followed by an Extraordinary General Meeting, held on 29 June 1860, to approve the sale of the company to the LBSCR. About this time, however, considerable trouble was being experienced with bad drainage of the track and for a time train loads of shingle were brought to the branch by two of the Newhaven based Longridge Goods 0-6-0 locomotives, Nos 104 and 106. Perhaps this accounts for the late acquisition of the line by the LBSCR in 1864 – or might it even have been the LBSCR's own financial problems of the period?

The timetable of January 1859 showed five passenger trains in each direction on weekdays and two on Sundays, all being worked from the Uckfield end. There was no scheduled goods service to begin with but this must have been introduced by 1861 when Billiter's siding was connected at Barcombe. By June 1864 there were six return passenger services in addition to an early morning goods train which worked to Lewes and back before the first passenger train each day. The last passenger train from Uckfield was actually listed as a mixed passenger and goods but there is no reference to this in the October timetable. In fact, by October 1864 there were seven return passenger services, all worked from the Uckfield end. The goods workings became an overnight service which returned to Uckfield the following morning and this pattern continued into 1866. By the middle of 1867, however, the service had been reduced to five passenger trains with one goods train each way.

A two-engine shed was provided at Uckfield for the branch line engines and on 22 February 1858 a small 2-4-0 tank locomotive, No 130, was ordered from Brighton Works especially for service on the branch. Although the opening date of the branch was delayed for a few weeks No 130 was still not complete and missed the ceremony by 10 days. It remained on the branch, however, until 1868 when the extension to Groombridge was completed and Uckfield shed closed. It was then transferred to Brighton and was often rostered to work the Kemp Town Branch which opened in 1869. Two small singles, numbered 137 and 138, were built at Brighton in 1859 and set to work from New Cross from 29 July but before long No 138 was recalled to Brighton for service on the Uckfield branch. It is not clear how long it remained on the branch for it was damaged by fire at Tunbridge Wells on 11 February 1867, 18 months before there was a direct link with that station. One of Craven's re-builds, No 115, was transferred to the branch some time after 1864 to share the duties with No 130. This engine started life as No 117, a Jones single, which

An undated image from Southern Railway days. This time it shows Station Master G. W. Kellow in the centre. Porter George Browning is on the left.

Courtesy John and Mary Browning

the LBSCR took over from the London & Brighton Railway and re-numbered 39 in 1845. It was re-numbered 34 in 1848 and 115 in 1849 and it was rebuilt as an 0-4-2 in October 1858, although it had been condemned to be broken up in July of that year. It was re-built again as an 0-4-2 tank in 1863 and worked between Hailsham and Eastbourne before being transferred to Uckfield. Apart from a couple of months at the end of 1868, when it was on loan to the Hayling Island Railway, it continued to work in the area after the link to Groombridge was completed. It suffered some minor damage at that station on 15 December 1858. Another locomotive which worked the line for some years during this decade was No 111 (previously No 84), one of the Sharps Long-Boiler 2-4-0s of 1847.

Powers to construct the Lewes and Uckfield Junction line were obtained by the LBSCR in 1864. When complete, the three and a half miles of double track linking with the Uckfield line at Hamsey would enable trains from Uckfield to enter Lewes from the eastern end of the station. While this was under construction the branch from Hamsey to Uckfield was doubled and the single line extension to Groombridge was under way. At the same time a fourth project, the Ouse Valley line, was also under construction and the deposited plans show the route from Haywards Heath curving north to join the Uckfield line just south of Uckfield station which, of course, was being rebuilt as a through station. Immediately north of the station the Ouse Valley line would have diverged to the east towards Hellingly before turning south to Hailsham to form an end-on junction with the branch from Polegate. The Ouse Valley line was abandoned and powers to that end were obtained in 1868 when the first three projects were completed. On 1 June 1868 the Board of Trade were sent three separate requests for inspections of the works with the intention of bringing them all into use on 1 July and, at the same time, closing the Hamsey loop to the Keymer line. In his reports, which were all dated 29 June, the Inspector, Colonel Yolland RE, found aspects which required further attention and although the Uckfield to Groombridge and Tunbridge Wells extension was able to open on 3 August the other two sections were delayed until 25 September 1868.

Loading timber at Uckfield on to bolster wagons and using the yard crane at the west end of the goods shed. *Courtesy John and Mary Browning*

The staff taking a break during the loading of a particularly heavy tree trunk at Uckfield with the yard crane. *Courtesy John and Mary Browning*

The mobile (wagon-mounted) crane used to supplement the yard crane at Uckfield, seen here loading timber. After World War 2, when the yard crane finally collapsed from old age, BR imported a tractor-mounted replacement, which is recalled as usually refusing to work at all!
Courtesy John and Mary Browning

It is felt that the reports of Colonel Yolland are of sufficient interest to be quoted in full:

LEWES & UCKFIELD JUNCTION RAILWAY

'Railway Department Board of Trade Whitehall 29th June 1868.

'Sir, I have the honour to report for the information of the Board of trade, that, in obedience to your minute of the 22nd instant, I have inspected the Lewes and Uckfield Junction Railway, between Hamsey and Lewes Station, a length of 1 mile and 78.5 chains

'This Line is double throughout, the width at formation Level is 30 feet and the gauge is 4 feet 8½ inches.

'The permanent way consists of a double headed rail that weighs 75 lbs per linear yard in lengths of 21 feet. Each length is supported in 8 cast iron chairs, six of which weigh 25 lbs each, with one near each end weighing 28 lbs each. The chairs are fastened to the 8 transverse sleepers by wrought iron spikes 6 inches long ¾ inch in diameter, driven through hard wooden compressed oak treenails. The rails are fixed in the chairs by compressed oak treenails placed outside the rails. The joints are fished with 2 plates each 18" long, bolted together with 4, ¾ inch bolts, with square shoulders and square heads and nuts. The sleepers are of Baltic Timber, rectangular 9 feet long by 10" x 5". they are said to be mostly creosoted.

'The bottom ballast is of chalk and the top ballast of gravel. The whole thickness is said to be about 2 feet in depth below the level of the rail.

'The sharpest curve on the line has a radius of 15 chains and the steepest incline is 1 in 50 close to the junction with the main lines at Lewes Station

'There are 3 over and 6 under Bridges in addition to 2 Viaducts. The Over bridges are entirely constructed in Brickwork. The Under Bridges and Viaducts are either entirely constructed in Brickwork, or with Brick abutments and wrought or Cast iron Girders – with in some instances Cast iron pillars resting on screw piles for piers. The whole of these works are well constructed and apparently sufficiently strong, but I have not yet got the details of one of these under bridges to calculate the strength. Where the rails are laid on Longitudinal Timbers, transomes with strap bolts to keep the gauge are required at every 11 feet – and where the rails are supported in bracket chairs, these chairs must be secured to the sleepers by fang bolts instead of coach screws.

'The main Line from London to Hastings crosses the Line from Brighton to Tunbridge Wells at Lewes Station and the latter descends to the Station on a very steep incline of 1 in 50. In the 2 forks the Company have sidings, Turntable and Goods yard. The Signal arrangements at the present time are incomplete, and they are to be so completed that is shall not be possible for anything to come out from either fork, on to the Main lines, without the special sanction of the Signalman, and he will be prevented mechanically from allowing anything to come out when he has any signal off for the admission of any Train to the Station. It is a particularly dangerous Station and the utmost care will be necessary in perfecting these arrangements.

'I have now therefore to report that the opening of the Lewes and Uckfield Junction Line for Traffic, cannot, by reason of the incompleteness of the works, be sanctioned without danger to the Public using the same.

'I have the honour to be, Sir Your Most Obedient Servant, J.M. Yolland Colonel'

'Brighton 28th July 1868.

'Sir, I have the honour to state for the information of the Board of Trade, that, in obedience to your minute of the 16th instant, I have re-inspected the Lewes and Uckfield Junction Railway; and to report that the London Brighton and South Coast Railway Company have not yet been enabled to complete the arrangements by which anything shall be prevented from coming out from the two forks formed by the London to Hastings Line crossing the Brighton to Tunbridge Wells Line, at Lewes Station without the special sanction of the Signalman and I have therefore to report that the opening of the Lewes and Uckfield Junction Line for Traffic, cannot by reason of the incompleteness of the works, be sanctioned without danger to the Public using the same.

'I have the honour to be, Sir Your Most Obedient Servant, J.M. Yolland Colonel'

'Railway Department Board of Trade Whitehall 23rd September 1868.

'Sir, I have the honour to state for the information of the Board of Trade, that, in obedience to your minute of the 19th instant, I have re-inspected the Lewes and Uckfield Junction Railway, between Hamsey and Lewes Station, and have to report that the whole of my requirements have now been complied with, and this railway may now be opened for Public Traffic.

'Slight alterations are immediately to be made in the locking of the points and Signals connected with the Goods Siding and Goods Crossing which join the down line from Lewes to Hastings South and East of the Station and a cross over road immediately outside this Siding is to be taken out altogether, prior to the opening taking place.

'I have the honour to be, Sir Your Most Obedient Servant, J.M. Yolland Colonel'

SECOND LINE OF RAILS – UCKFIELD JUNCTION TO UCKFIELD

'Railway Department Board of Trade Whitehall 29th June 1868.

'Sir, I have the honour to report for the information of the Board of trade, that, in obedience to your minute of the 22nd instant, I have inspected the 2nd line of rails between Hamsey and Uckfield on the Lewes and Uckfield Branch of the London Brighton and South Coast Railway. The precise length of this portion of line is not stated in the details, but it is somewhat more than 6 miles in length.

'The permanent way is similar to that laid down in the first line of rails, and it is described in the accompanying diagram. It is good and substantial, and the line is in good order, but the girders of a bridge at 2m 33ch from the junction at Hamsey, of cast iron for a span of 27 feet, are too weak.

'Improvements are required in connexion with the Signals Points Sidings and Level Crossings at Uckfield, Barcombe and Isfield Stations by which the sidings will terminate in blind sidings, the facing points leading from them, as well as points of cross over roads being locked by the signals, when taken off for Trains to enter the Stations.

'Arrangements are also to be made by which the Gates at the Level Crossings are to be prevented from being opened when the Signals are off, for a Train to enter the Station. Clocks visible from the Platforms are required. I have now therefore to report, that by reason of the incompleteness of the works, the opening of the second Line of Rails between Hamsey and Uckfield for traffic cannot be sanctioned without danger to the public using the same.

'I have the honour to be, Sir, Your most obedient Servant, YOLLAND Colonel'

'Brighton 28th July 1868

'I have the honour to report for the information of the Board of Trade, that, I have in obedience to our minute

The level crossing and signal box at Uckfield c1935. The station was on the south side of the level crossing, a roadway which has become ever more congested in recent times. Post 1969 the railway south of Uckfield to Lewes was closed and in 1991 a new terminus station was opened 55 yards to the north, so allowing the crossing to be closed.

of the 16th instant, re-inspected the 2nd line of line (rails) between Hamsey and Uckfield Station on the Lewes and Uckfield Branch of the London Brighton and South Coast railway and to report that the girders of an under bridge at 2m 33ch from the Junction at Hamsey have been strengthened by the introduction of intermediate iron supports midway between the abutments without materially interfering with the amount of the waterway.

'The arrangements have not yet been completed by which the gates at the Level crossings at Isfield and Barcombe Stations are prevented from being opened, when the Signals are off for a Train to Enter the Station and I have therefore to report that the opening of the second line of rails between Hamsey and Uckfield Stations for traffic cannot be sanctioned without danger to the public using the same.

'I have the honour to be Sir Your Most Obedient Servant, J.M. Yolland Colonel'

'Railway Department Board of Trade, Whitehall 23rd September 1868.

'Sir, I have the honour to state for the information of the Board of Trade, that, in obedience to your minute of the 19th instant, I yesterday re-inspected the second Line of Rails, between Hamsey and Uckfield Station, and to report that the whole of my requirements have now been complied with and there is no longer any objection to the opening of this Line for Public Traffic it being understood that the first Line of Rails is to be entirely disconnected at Hamsey with that portion lying between the Junction with the main Line London to Lewes and Hamsey and connected with the Second Line of Rails of the Lewes and Uckfield Junction Railway.

'I have the honour to be Sir Your Most Obedient Servant, J.M. Yolland Colonel'

UCKFIELD TO GROOMBRIDGE

'Railway Department, Board of Trade, Whitehall, 29th June, 1868.

'Sir, I have the honour to report for the information of the Board of trade, that, in obedience to your minute of the 22nd instant, I have inspected that portion of the Brighton, Uckfield and Tunbridge Wells Railway, situated between Groombridge and Uckfield stations, a length of 12 miles and 20 chains.

'This line is laid single throughout with sidings at each of the stations, but is otherwise constructed for a double line with the exception of the Permanent way and Ballasting.

'The width of the line at formation level is 30 feet and the gauge is 4 feet 8½ inches.

Double headed rails that weigh 75 lbs per linear yard, laid in lengths of 21 feet, are made use of. Each length is supported by 8 cast iron chairs, six of which weigh 25 lbs each, with one near each end, next but one to the joint, weighing 28 lbs each. The chairs are fastened to transverse sleepers eight to each length of 21 feet, by wrought iron spikes, 6 inches long ¾ inch in diameter, driven through compressed oak treenails. Each 25 lbs chair has 2 and each 28 lbs chair 3 spikes. The rails are fixed in the chairs by compressed oak keys placed outside the rails. The joints are fished with 2 plates each 18 inches long, bolted together with 4¾ inch bolts with square shoulders and square heads and nuts. The sleepers are of Baltic Timber, said to be mostly creosoted, 9 feet long by 10" wide & 5" deep.

'The Ballast is of gravel and chalk each said to be 12 inches deep.

'The sharpest curve on the Line has a radius of 30 chains and the steepest incline is 1in 754. There are 3 stations on the Line – Eridge, Rotherfield and Buxted and there are Engine Turntables at Tunbridge Wells, Uckfield, Lewes and Brighton, but I was informed that the turntable at Uckfield was to be removed and the traffic worked through between Tunbridge Wells and Lewes, if not from Brighton.

'There are 8 over and 22 under bridges besides 2 viaducts respectively of 191 and 177 yards in length – these last are important works constructed of brickwork in mortar with 11 arches in one and 10 in the other, each of 40 feet span well constructed so that I only noticed that there had been a very slight settlement over the Southernmost pier of the first Viaduct called Sleeches – and that not to any extent.

'The over and under bridges are partly constructed in timber, partly in brickwork, but mostly with brickwork and Cast Iron Girders. There is also one bridge with Wrought Iron Girders with an opening of 46⅔ feet. All are sufficiently strong – as far as one line of way is in question. There is also a tunnel of 1,020 yards in length lined throughout with brickwork and with four shafts. There is a good deal of water still falling through parts of this tunnel.

'1. There have been some heavy slips in the embankments which will require to be looked after. There are a good many things to attend to on this Line. The Permanent way over many of the under Girder bridges is not properly laid. The rails are supported on bracket chairs fixed to planking over longitudinal Timbers by coach screws for which bolts with a nut on top or fang bolts should be substituted. The Girders require tie rods at each end and Longitudinal Timbers have to be laid down across these openings under the rails and these also will require transomes and tie rods in order to keep the gauge.

'2. The line wants lifting, regulating and packing especially close to the abutments of these bridges: and additional ballast is required. The fencing is also deficient in places along the Line pointed out to the Engineer and a good many fish bolts are not in.

'3. At Groombridge Station the points were not properly put in, and the Engine twice mounted the rails in consequence. The signal arrangements were incomplete and an additional blind siding is required with a signal in connexion the Goods yard, the facing points with interlocking with the Junction Signals and thus preventing anything coming out of the yard when the other signals are off.

'4. At the three stations the points for entering or coming out from the sidings require to be locked by the signals, when these are taken off for the arrival or passing of any train.

'5. Clocks are required at the stations, visible on the platforms. Station names are also required.

[There is no mention of No 6.]

'7. There are some spikes and obstructions in the tunnel to be removed to allow the door of a van to be opened.

Uckfield signal box taken in November 1960 with the River Uck in flood. Signalman Fred Hunt is on duty and it was noted the structure was still in standard green and cream style. The steps seen were later moved to the opposite east end, intended to make room for new level crossing barriers although these were never installed.

'I have now therefore to report that by reason of the incompleteness of the works the opening of the Brighton, Uckfield and Tunbridge Wells Railway between Uckfield and Groombridge for traffic cannot be sanctioned without danger to the Public using the same.'

'Brighton, 29th July, 1868.

'Sir, I have the honour to state for the information of the Board of Trade, that, in obedience to your minute of the 16th instant, I have re-inspected the portion of the Brighton Uckfield and Tunbridge Wells line situated between Groombridge and Uckfield stations and I have to report that the requirements detailed in my report of Inspection dated the 29th Ult'. have now been complied with and the sanction of the Board of Trade to the opening of this single line may be given as soon as a satisfactory undertaking of the mode of working the line has been received. I understand that it is to be worked on the train staff and ticket system with the exception of the length between Rotherfield and Buxted Stations, where on account of the Rotherfield Tunnel, only one Train is to be permitted on the line between these stations at one and the same time. The Electric Telegraph has been laid down between these stations and two of Tyers Instruments are to be employed in order to work this length on the block system.

'I have the honour to be
Sir Your most obedient servant Yolland Colonel.'

(The punctuation is that of Colonel Yolland)

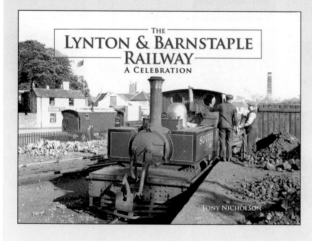

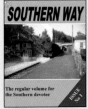

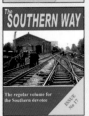

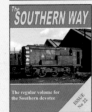
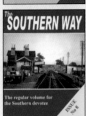
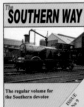

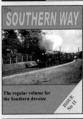

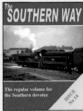

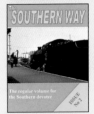

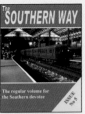

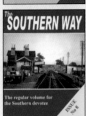

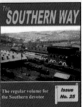
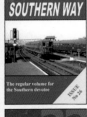

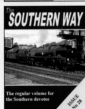
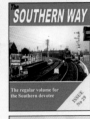

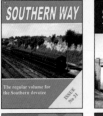
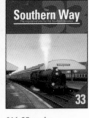
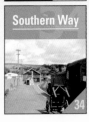

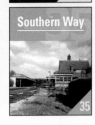
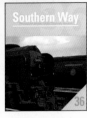
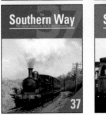
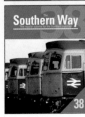
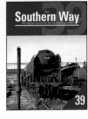